GREEN STAR OVER WEST BENGAL

GREEN STAR OVER WEST BENGAL

Study of Mamata Banerjee

Surajit Kumar Dasgupta

KALPAZ

Published by

Kalpaz Publications
C-30, Satyawati Nagar,
Delhi – 110052
Ph.: 011-47034999, 9811692060
www.kalpazpublications.com
E-mail: kalpaz@hotmail.com

Distribution Network
gyanbooks.com
India, USA, Canada, UK, Australia, France

ISBN: 978-93-5722-503-8 (PB)

First Published, 2024

Printed at: Gyan Press, Delhi.

Green Star Over West Bengal: Study of Mamata Banerjee
Author: Surajit Kumar Dasgupta

CONTENTS

PREFACE

The highly spirited and dynamic lady Mamata Banerjee was born in Calcutta on 5th January 1955. She is the daughter of Promileswar Banerjee, a government contractor and freedom-fighter whose brief life oscillated between periodic spells of affluence and penury and it was terminated at the age of fortyone. Her mother Gayatri Devi had instilled in her mind at an early age the spirit of justice and fairplay, deep feeling for all human beings and the courage to stand for the downtrodden.

Simplicity and austerity and uprightness are the hallmarks of her turbulent political career and dynamic moral character. Not unlike America's Clara Jetkin, Europe's Joan of Arc, Orissa's Nandini Satpathi and India's illustrious Indira Gandhi from her early childhood days, she had been an intrepid and intelligent lady who believes in the equality of sexes and displayed pronounced leadership qualities and organising abilities. All along she had been an uncompromising crusader against all sorts of social and political injustices and oppressions. Her life-history is a consistent account of immaculate altruism, self-abnegation and high idealism, coupled with indomitable elan and will power to bring about transformation in an unjust and obsolete polity economy and society.

In the last 34 years what did she not have to tolerate in the 'hell of crimes' the leftist West Bengal? Everything, from personal character assassination to physical aggression is the answer. In 1991 at the Hazra crossing the rod of a Lalu Alam a C P(M) miscreant almost snatched away her life. In 1994 when she was herself a minister in the national government the barbarous police forces of the left front chief minister Jyotl Basu of West Bengal literally caught hold of her by hairs and threw her out of Writers Building by force.

This was in fact an act of gross misbehaviour and vandalism

and violation of all norms of civilized conduct and sobriety. It was highly unbecoming of an old man like Jyoti Basu. Nonetheless the Central Government remained unconcerned and Jyoti Basu was not brought to book. The seemingly incurable reluctance to use the security forces on the part of Mamata Banerjee was also partly responsible for this disaster. The 'mulish' and uncultured gesture of then Minister for Cultural Affairs Buddhadev Bhattacharya and the obnoxious and pejorative utterances of senior leaders of CPM like Benoy Konar and Anil Basu constitute a dark chapter in the discredited history of the left front rule in west Bengal.

Ultimately out of disgust Mamata Banerjee came out of Congress and formed her own party Trinamool Congress in 1997. Today she has turned out to be victorious in her struggle against her arch enemy CPM.

All these years she has continued her struggle against the injustices and oppressions of CPM in an uncompromising manner. In the final analysis she has succeded in her noble mission of winning the hearts of the masses. Her crusade in favour of the 'mother, earth and man' (MA-MATI-MANUSH) has at last been crowned with success. She has acquired the magical powers to attract the ordinary masses to her own viewpoint.

Today, she is not only a highly popular woman leader of the region but also the first woman chief minister of West Bengal. In the electoral warfare in 1984, in the leftist bastion of Jadavpur the veteran CP(M) leader Somnath Chatterjee was defeated at her hands. The entire left front turned turtle in the lands of the 'giant killer' who later converted the 'winds of change' into a cyclone.

She never indulged in opportunist politics. By virtue of her charismatic image she has ascended today the pinnacle of political powers in West Bengal. She was determined to drive out the left front from the political arena in West Bengal but that government has left for the government of the 'fire daughter' (agnikanya) the burden of a debt of two lakh crores of rupees. Now the big question before her is how Mamata Banerjee will solve the problem of rescuing West Bengal from this insolvent situation. Not only that this victory has significantly enlarged her image in national politics. There are many interesting stories behind this dramatic ascent and upheaval of Mamata Banerjee.

She holds Bachelors Degrees in Arts (Hons. in History), Education (B.Ed.), Law (L.LB) and Master's Degree (in Islamic History) from Calcutta University. She was a student of Jogamaya Devi College of South Calcutta, Shri Shikshyatan and Jogesh Chandra Chaudhuri College. She was inducted to the West Bengal Chhatra Parishad while a student of Jogamaya Devi College and worked as a member of the working Committee of Chhatra Parishad during 1977-1983. She held the position of General Secretary West Bengal Congress (Indira) from 1979-1980 and Secretary, West Bengal Provincial Trade Union Congress. During the period 1983-1988 she was the Secretary of the Women's wing of the Indian National Trade Union Congress and Secretary, South Calcutta District Congress (Indira) for the period 1980-1985. In 1984 she was elected as a Member of Parliament from Jadavpur Constituency and held the post of General Secretary of the Youth Congress (Indira) and became a member of the National Council in 1987 and a member of the Executive Committee in the Congress Parliamentary Party in 1988. She has got re-elected as a Member of Parliament in 1991, 1996, 1998, 1999, 2004 and 2009 from the South Kolkata Parliamentary Constituency making her one of India's most experienced Parliamentarians. She has been a member of several Parliamentary Committees.

Mamata Banerjee served as a Minister of Railways twice (1999 and 2009), Minister of Coal and Mines in 2004 and Minister of State for Human Resource Development, Department of Youth Affairs and Sports and Women and Child Development once in the cabinet of the Government of India.

She opposed forceful land acquisition for industrialization by the then Communist Government in West Bengal at Singur and Nandigram for Special Economic Zones (SEZ) at the cost of the agriculturists and farmers.

In 2011, All India Trinamool Congress registered a landslide victory defeating the world's longest serving democratically elected Communist government, the Communist Party Of India (Marxist) led Left Front government, bringing to an end a 34 year - old regime. On May 20, 2011 Mamata Banerjee took over as the first lady to be the chief minister of West Bengal.

She is the 11th chief minister and first woman chief minister of the region. The highlight of the election was that only four ministers out of the 28 of the outgoing regime were able to retain their seats. Even the outgoing chief minister Buddhadev Bhattacharya lost in his own constituency.

In spite of her very busy work schedule she has authored over 20 books and created over 5,000 oil paintings quite a few of which have been auctioned. The proceeds of such auctions have been donated by her to various social activities. Throughout her political life she maintained an austere lifestyle and never spent money on costly clothes, cosmetics and jewellery and slung a cotton bag on her shoulder. She has remained single throughout her life.

She is a widely travelled lady who represented the country in (i) U.N. General Assembly (ii) as a woman parliamentarian at World Women's Round Table Conference, Russia and (iii) World Youth Conference, Vietnam, (iv) attended the Working Women's Conference of ILO and ICFTU at Kualalumpur. She observed *dhama* in 1995 for 21 days to restore Human Rights and protested against atrocities on women and lock-up deaths in the country specially in West Bengal.

Kolkata - 700004 **SURAJIT KUMAR DAS GUPTA**

Acknowledgements

I am thankful to Subhrajyoti Barat for the careful typing of the entire manuscript and to my sister Sumitra, wife Gayatri and brothers-in-law Santosh Kumar Dasgupta and Prabir Roy for their unstinted help and co-operation during the writing of the book.

INTRODUCTION

In the Assembly election of 2001 Buddhadev Bhattacharya won in 199 seats and became the chief minister of West Bengal and gave three assurances. First, the 'Do it now' slogan to bring back work culture to the government departments. In other words, work should not be kept unfinished. Secondly, administration will be sensitive. In other words, the government will stand by the side of common man in their times of trials and tribulations. Thirdly, one of the objectives of the government will be to bring back 'transparency' to administration. People will be aware of everything. Taken all things together, a populist image of CP(M) was sought to be built up by the chief minister.

For understandable reasons, the question was raised then Jyoti Basu, who had been chief minister for 23 years and in whose ministry Buddhadev Bhattacharya remained from the very beginning, was doing what for this long period? From the relevant papers it was seen that after coming to power in 1977 Jyoti Basu also uttered almost similar words which Buddhadev Bhattacharya said after coming to power in 2001.

After becoming chief minister Buddhadev Bhattacharya made it clear that Jyoti Basu's left front government did not keep its promises. At the same time he also gave the assurance that performance will match the words during his administration which was given the highsounding title 'improved left front government'. In other words, the assurances of a change were given. In this year's election Trinamool Congress gave the same assurance of change in its manifesto in which are implicit those three declarations of Buddhadev Bhattacharya.

Today while taking stock of events, it is seen that Buddhadev Bhattaeharya was the fittest successor of Jyoti Basu, that is, a total failure. But the matter should not be concluded here. Rather, the government of 'mother-earth-and-man' can take lessons from the failure of its predecessor.

Today in order to draw its graph of success the story of the failure of Buddhadev Bhattacharya is most pertinent. He promised that he would not step into the shoes of Jyoti Basu. His failure in keeping that promise is directly proportional to the success in achieving the targets by Mamata Banerjee.

In 2005 Mamata Banerjee protested against the forceful land acquisition and the atrocities on local farmers in the name of industrial development policy of the Left front Government in West Bengal. Benny Santosa, CEO of the Indonesia-based Salim Group had pledged a large investment to West Bengal and the West Bengal Government had given him farmland in Howrah, sparking protest.

Mamata Banerjee suffered further setbacks in 2005 when her party lost control of the Kolkata Municipal Corporation and the sitting Mayor defected from her party. In 2006 the Trinamool Congress was defeated in West Bengal's Assembly elections losing more than half of its sitting members.

In 2006 the Tata Nano Singur controversy took place. It was generated by the Nano factory of Tata Motors at Singur in the Hooghly district. Singur gained international media attention since Tata Motors started constructing a factory to manufacture their $2500 car, the Tata Nano at Singur. The small car was scheduled to roll out of the factory by 2008. The regional government of West Bengal facilitated the controversy by using an old rule of 1897 to conduct an eminent domain takeover of 997 acres of farmland to have Tata build its factory. The rule is meant for public improvement projects and the West Bengal government wanted Tata to build its factory in its own region. Opponents included displaced farmers and Land-rights people.

The choice of Singur was made by the company among six sites offered by the regional government. The project faced massive opposition from displaced farmers. The unwilling farmers were given political support by West Bengal's opposition leader Mamata Banerjee whose 'Save Farmland' movement was supported by environmental activists and intellectuals like Medha Patkar, Anuradha Talwar and Arundhuti Roy. Mamata's movement against displacement of farmers was also supported by several kolkata based celebrities like Aparna Sen, Kaushik Sen, Shaonli Mitra and Suva Prasanna. Ultra left activists also shared the platform with Mamata Banerjee's Trinamool Party.

In the 1950s West Bengal was one of the most industrialized regions in the country. Bidhan Roy its first chief minister founded large industrial plants in Durgapur, Asansol, Kalyani and Howrah and Calcutta proper. In the 1960s and 1970s disruptions by the Bangladesh war, the Naxal movement and militant trade unionism by leftist parties led by Jyoti Basu slowed down industrial development.

Consequently, other regions such as Maharashtra, Gujarat, Punjab, Tamil Nadu and Karnataka attracted industrial investment and experienced job growth. The rapid rise in the population of West Bengal has not been accompained by significant economic growth. Key indicators such as unemployment rates, poverty rates, infant mortality rates, job growth rates, per capita income, mobile phone penetration rates lag behind the more industrialized regions of India.

Local politicians gained power by promising agricultural land to landless farmers, but given West Bengal's population density, the land-holdings are small and the yields are insufficient to sustaion poor families. While the shift from agricultural to industrial jobs require retraining given its economic growth *it* provides an opportunity for earning higher income.

The people staying in the proposed land were forced to evacuate by the government.The compensation given was considered inadequate and the new housing facilities were delayed. This led to the protest of the peasants backed by opposition political parties who thought it would be a good opportunity to end the Communist rule.

The company has made substantial promises. According to their claims Singur would become a mini-auto city and approximately 70 vendors would set up shops along with the factory. The total investment planned is to the tune of Rs.1000 crores. The project had however generated controversy right from the start particularly on the question of government acquisition of fertile agricultural land for private enterprise.

The Nobel Laureate Amartya Sen defended the decision to set up the factory. The protesters have been trenchantly attacked, verbally by the CP(M) leaders and physically by the party's succesors. However in the 2011 Assembly elections while the sitting Trinamool Congress MLA Rabindranath Bhattacharya retained the Singur seat, Becharam Manna, the convener of Krishi Jami Raksha Samiti won the adjoining Haripal seat.

While the ruling party went all out for acquisition of 997 acres (404 ha) of multicrop land required for the car factory, questions were raised about the party's forcible acquisition which was made under the Colonial Land Acquisition Act of 1894.

Some said that the provisions of this Act were allegedly not met. The Law had provisions for government taking over privately held land for public purposes but not for development of private business. The illegality of the acquisition was substantially conceded by the Kolkata High Court. The Tata Motors site is the most fertile one in the whole of Singur and the Singur Block, in turn, is among the most highly fertile in West Bengal. Consequently, almost the entire local populace depends on agriculture with approximately 15,000 making their livelihood directly from it. With the number of direct jobs to be created no more than about 1,000, many of which were expected to go to outsiders, the local populace felt understandably threatened for their livelihood. Environmental degradation was also feared. Chief protesters included the opposition parties spearheaded by the Trinamool Congress under Mamata Banerjee and Socialist Unity Centre of India.

The land earmarked for the project was taken control of by the government administration amidst protests and fencing off commenced on December 1,2006. Mamata Banerjee who was prevented from entering Singur by the police called a state wide bandh in protest. Later she went on a 25-day hunger strike. The fenced off area was regularly guarded by cadres of the CP(M) party besides large contingents of policemen. They were accused of the multiple rape followed by turning to death of teenage villager Tapasi Malik who was active in the protests, on December 18, 2006. Negligence and political interference in the probe into her death were alleged. Later CP(M) activist Debu Malik and based on his statement CP(M) Zonal Committee Secretary Suhrid Datta were arrested by the Central Bureau of Investigation in connection with the crime.

Other aspects of the process of setting up the factory that came under severe criticism were the government's secrecy on the details of the deal and the chief minister's furnishing of false information in the Bidhan Sabha. In particular, the concessions being given to Tata Motors have not been publicly revealed.

The falsehoods of the chief minister pertain to claims made by him of having acquired 912 acres (3.69 km^2) through voluntary consent of the owners without the use of force. In 2007, the government admitted that 30 percent of the land was acquired from farmers without consent. It remained unclear whether the lack of consent was based on insufficiency of compensation or refusal to sell altogether.

Tatas ceremonially initiated the construction of the plant on 21 January, 2007. They announced on October 3, 2008 that they are pulling off Singur due to the political agitation and unrest by the Trinamool Congress against the construction of the plant. On 7th October, 2008 the Tatas announced that they would be setting up the Tata Nano Plant in Sanand, Gujarat.

While going to follow the 'Do-it-now' principle people like Buddhadev Bhattacharya and Nirupam Sen etc. ignored the government regulations and went to acquire land to build a chemical hub (SEZ) at Nandigram in East Midnapore district, resulting in the killing of 14 villagers in police firing. Trinamool Congress staged blockade, protests and strikes. The left front government shelved the proposed chemical hub project.

The Bengalees understood that Buddhadev Bhattacharya was not only a crafty political leader but also an expert actor. After the killing incident in Nandigram he admitted that he was alone responsible for the whole thing but he did not give up power. Nor did he punish the guilty police officers. And again in the last lap of the electoral propaganda he claimed that 'I did not give the order of firing. Nor did I know that the police will open fire.

But from the flow of events it is clear that firing was done to smash the Nandigram movement at the clearcut directives of the authorities of Writers's Building and Alimuddin Street. In the following period Buddhadev's administration has ignored the directives of the High Court and the Human Rights Commission and day after day neglected to pay compensation to the families of the dead and the wounded persons. It indicates that 'sensitivity' was never a strong point of his administration. Shamelessly he converted Writers Building into his party office and supported the armed attacks of his party activists on the unarmed villagers and reoccupying Nandigram. Shamelessly he declared that 'they have been paid back in their own coins'.

During the last lap of his ministership Benoy Chowdhury said that the government was being conducted by the contractors in the interest of the contractors. Benoy babu was a symbol of honesty and the second person in Jyoti Basu's ministry Benoy babu's words are more applicable to the ten years of administration of Buddhadev Bhattacharya. All the government offices including the Writers Buildings have become converted into the heavens of the contractors, promoters and the brokers of the industrialists. The direction of administration was towards the affluent section of the society and Buddhadev's role in this matter was significant. On the one hand he has instigated his officers to procure land for the Tatas, Salims and Jindals and on the other hand owing to unavailability of land hundreds of crores of rupees alloted by the Centre for the building of houses of poor people in Indira Avas yojana and Ambedkar Yojana have been returned to the national government.

As regards transparency as well, Buddhadev's administration was a sad failure. He never disclosed the government's contracts with the Tatas about Singur, with the Salims about the chemical hubs at Nandigram and with the Jindals about the Shalbani Steel Plant. Secrecy was the hard malady of his government.

Despite great failures Buddhadev Bhattacharya continued to be the chief minister for 10 years, Mamata Banerjee has no comparable party organisation. But this very fact may be the keystick of her success. She does not have to think of the party at every step.

Because hers is the last word in her party. If she can utilise this seemingly undemocratic organization for the purpose of public welfare, it will indeed create a new chapter in the history of West Bengal.

PART-I

(MAY - SEPTEMBER 2011)

1

GREEN STAR OVER WEST BENGAL

In the month of April 1975 the Special Branch of Calcutta Police first opened a file in the name of the youngest politician in West Bengal and commented in her name: 'the most aggressive political leader'. Her name was Mamata Banerjee. In the previous years she had been the Unit Secretary of the Student's Union of Jogamaya Devi College. Since then she was regarded as a frontranking Congress leader of South Calcutta. However at that time very few people believed that the young lady who had just then become the convenor of the South Calcutta Mahila Congress in 1976 will turn out to be a giant-killer within only eight years and ultimately become a Member of Parliament. Thereafter in 1997 she left the Congress and formed her own new party. Everybody had the impression that she would end in becoming a total failure. In 2004 and 2006 the election results were miserable. But she was undaunted and did not give up all hopes.

Mamata Banerjee, the Cinderella of Indian politics had been continuously humiliated by being marginalised within her own party but did not totally break down. In the Loksabha election of 2004 she was victorious only in her own seat and day after day she sat totally alone as a single member party in the Parliament. The leftist MPs hurled ridicules at her and excited her by uttering ugly words. She was hindered at every step in delivering her own speech. With her own eyes she had witnessed the camaraderie between CP(M) and the Congress. Wiping the tears of her eyes she had left the parliament House but never gave up all hopes.

This transition in the life of Mamata Banerjee is today the inspiration for many people. Through sheer talent and tenacity or hard labour she has demolished the red bastion of 34 years' rule of

CP(M) and become the green star in the political firmament of West Bengal almost by her single-handed efforts. The allegory which started by selling Haringhata milk in a roadside depot of Kalighat ended at the assumption of political powers as the chief minister in the Writers Building.

Many of us have read the book entitled 'From Log-cabin to White House' which is concerned with the life of President Abraham Lincoln of America. The political upheaval of Mamata Banerjee is in many ways comparable to this meteoric rise of the American President. She belongs to a lower middle class Bengali family and lacks the political or educational pedigrees of any of her predecessors.

Two of her most memorable political achievements are: in the first place she came out of the Congress, built up her own party almost single handed, rose to the apex of the regional politics and established her party in the second position in the arena of New Delhi politics. Secondly, she smashed down almost single handed a cadre-based political machinery like CP(M). It was she who proved in the last 34 years to the residents of West Bengal that CP(M) was not invincible and that it can also be defeated.

How could Mamata Banerjee achieve these two extraordinary political successes? Mamata Banerjee succeeded in these two objectives by virtue of her personal integrity, her sincere and unflinching efforts in an uncompromising struggle against CP(M) and her facile ability to mix with and move among the ordinary citizens. It is these ordinary citizens who remain throughout at the very centre of all her political activities. That is why she received in return the unstinted and inexhaustible support of the common men. Undoubtedly, her qualities are admirable and rare in contemporary Indian politics.

Not that Mamata Banerjee was the first person to rebel against the Congress and form a party of her own. Many people before her did it and will also do the same in future. But how many among them could achieve such spectacular and historic success? Let us first have a look at regional politics. In 1967, Ajoy Mukherjee severed all connections with Congress and fought the election after constituting his own Bangla Congress. By holding the hands of the leftists it was possible for him to receive instantaneous success. Mukherjee's personal integrity, past political tradition and his role in the freedom struggle were above all suspicions and possible criticism. But not unlike a comet his Bangla Congress all on a sudden appeared and disappeared in the political firmament of West Bengal. In 1977 the veteran Gandhian leader Prafulla Chandra Sen who was the ex-chief minister of West Bengal left Congress and became a leader of the Janata Party in West Bengal but failed to estabilish that party on a strong foothold in the regional politics. By their centrifugal movement outside the mainstream of Congress both the leaders faced the end of their political careers. The political pedigree of Mamata Banerjee cannot certainly be compared with those of Ajoy Mukherjee and Prafulla Chandra Sen.

Pranab Mukherjee once left Congress and formed his own Rashtriya Samajbadi Congress. Along with him there was Gundu Rao of Karnataka. In the Assembly vote of 1987 the deposits of all the candidates of that party of Pranabbabu were confiscated by going out of the Congress Party. Nobody among Ajoy Mukherjee, Prafulla Sen or Pranab Mukherjee could establish their own parties on a strong foothold, not to say anything about rising at the vertex of popularity in the regional politics and dislodging the ruling CP(M) from the pedestal of political power unlike Mamata Banerjee.

At the first half of the seventies at the all-India level leaders like Morarji Desai and Jagjivan Ram came out of Congress and formed the Congress (Organization) but failed to give it or its successor Janata Party a long span of life. Although they suceeded in dislodging Indira Gandhi from power, it was only a temporary occurrence. At the end of the seventies in the year 1978-1979, men like Devraj Urs, K. Brahmananda Reddy, Y.B. Chavan, A.K. Anthony, Sharad Pawar, Priyaranjan Dasmunshi, Sharat Chandra Sinha etc. broke away from the Congress (I) and at first formed Congress (Urs) and thereafter Congress (S) or Congress (Socialist) but all these were totally transient happenings. In course of time with the exception of Saratbabu all the other persons eventually returned to the mainstream of Congress. In 1987-1988 keeping V.P. Singh in the forefront Arun Nehru, Ashok Sen, Arif Mohammed Khan etc. left the Congress of Rajiv Gandhi and at first formed the Jan Morcha and thereafter Janata Dal but failed to lengthen its life span.

Very recently in 1998 i.e. within one year of the formation of

Trinamool Congress by Mamata Banerjee men like Sharad Pawar and Purna Sangma came out of Congress and formed in 1999 the Nationalist Congress Party (NCP). Within thirteen years Mamata Banerjee succeeded in uprooting a so-called organized party like CP(M) from power and established her own party Trinamool Congress in power in West Bengal almost by her lone efforts. But this is what Sharad Pawar failed to do in Maharashtra. Also in the arena of national politics Sharad Pawar's NCP is lagging much behind Trinamool Congress of Mamata Banerjee.

This is where Mamata Banerjee is superior to all the others. Because they left the Congress owing to a fight of ego over personal image. Ajoy Mukherjee had troubles with Prafulla Chandra Sen. And starting from Prafulla Chandra Sen, Morarji Desai, V.P. Singh and very recently Sharad Pawar and Purna Sangma had either conflict of ego with Indira Gandhi or personal differences with Rajiv Gandhi or sought to serve their own narrow personal political interests in the grab of fighting on the sham excuse of foreign citizenship of Sonia Gandhi by birth and left Congress on that account. On the other hand Mamata Banerjee left Congress solely for the sake of conducting an uncompromising crusade against CP(M). Because her allegation was that the West Bengal Pradesh Congress was not sincere in their fight against CP(M). Like melons they are green outside but red inside. She called them 'tarmuz congress' who have sold themselves to the CP(M). Mamata forsook the company of Congress (I) and formed her own party Trinamool Congress because she was convinced that even the Congress High Comm and was not sincerely interested in fighting an uncompromising battle against CP(M) in West Bengal. Even today she is confirmed in that conviction and conflict. Her personal integrity is above anybody's suspicion.

Mamata Banerjee has held ministerial positions in the national government in more than one phases. She was also the Railways Minister once before. But taking advantage of the Ministry in the national government she did not become another A.Raja or Sukhram. Even today we can see that she does not believe in the blind allegiance to the party. Her vision is not befogged by a division between 'We and They' and she feels comfortable in the midst of the crowds of men. It was Mao Ze-Dong who used to aver that Communists must always remain among the people just as fishes abound in water. In a like manner Mamata Banerjee is seen to be comfortable in the midst of human crowds. CP(M) and CP(I) however do not behave in a like manner. Wearing a pair of hawai chappals Mamata Banerjee can walk miles after miles in a procession. On the other hand the CP(M) and CP(I) leaders can not walk even a single furlong.

This is the second keystick of the political success of Mamata Banerjee. She demolished CP(M) in West Bengal. She closed down the shutters of Buddhadev Bhattacharya & Co. in West Bengal.

The CP(M) activists are free to heap their ridicules over her as the 'fire-daughter' (Agnikanya) of Patuapara but the miserable defeat of this large party in her hands is an undeniable fact of history.

The familiar socio-economic circumstances of the lower middle class Bengalee tinshed which was the nursing home of the cadres of the Communist Party and the origin of the political support and the votebank of the undivided CPI at first and CP(M) thereafter also gave birth to Mamata Banerjee. She was not born with a silver spoon in her mouth. Unlike Dr. Bidhan Chandra Roy, Siddharthashankar Roy or Jyoti Basu she had no familial political or educational pedigree. She is not the niece of any famous poet. She was never a student of Presidency College. She never went to U.K. to become a barrister. She did not have higher education unlike the first chief minister of West Bengal, Dr. Prafulla Chandra Ghosh. Unlike Prafulla Chandra Sen or Ajoy Mukherjee she did not have any firsthand experience of working as an apprentice of Gandhian politics. On the contrary she had once the hard life of working as an ordinary employee of Haringhata milk depot. Such a person could easily become a cadre of the Communist Party. But the irony of fate is that incourse of time she proved to be the nemesis of the biggest political party in West Bengal CP(M).

No one knows for certain what Mamata Banerjee will become in the future years. For the simple reason that there is no last word in politics. Already the international opinion is highly optimistic about her probable future career. However if she persists in her humanist conduct like today, if she remains unflinching in her own political convictions and determination, if she is not over-whelmed with the intoxication of chief ministership in the Writers Building, if she also does not, like her adversaries, go to acquire farming lands on the pretext of industrial development, if she can expedite the progress of her own region, at least to some extent her name will ultimately be inscribed in letters of gold in the hearts of the umpteen millions of this region for ever and her image will continue to shine as the green star over the political horizons of West Bengal.

2

STRATEGY OF DEVELOPMENT - 1

The 'package' which the chief minister Mamata Banerjee announced in Jangalmahal has demonstrated a holistic approach to development. Employment, vocational training, improvement of the educational system at all levels, improvement of the standard of health services and improvement of the transport system-all these facets have been emphasised in her declaration. There is little doubt that for the rapid development of any area these matters are essential and over and above that, for the sake of establishment of social justice such efforts are indispensable. The increase in the number of old age allowances, rice at a subsidised rate, conveyance of medical treatment to the remote villages through the bike-driving health activists-all these initiatives will help the poorest people to live with dignity.

The question may of course be raised how all such matters may be arranged within a short period? Jangalmahal is neglected for long and by taking advantage of this phenomenon, the Maoist movement had broken out in this area. An adequate environment is needed for constructing colleges, health centres and factories and to keep them in an on-going position. How can new institutions be started where many schools had been remaining closed for long? Then again what will be the gain by building a centre for cultural exercise within a climate of terrorism? When the public treasury of the region has been exhausted, it is also difficult to provide the finance for these huge development activities. Then again how can one ignore the likelihood that the finance for development after coming to Jangalmahal will be squandered amidst various channels of corrupt activities?

All these are important misgivings but not the most important questions. In her visit to Nayagram and Jhargram the new chief minister has explained to the people at large how she desires to solve the problems of Jangalmahal and what are her designs and strategy. After her declaration it has been evident that she is looking upon socio-economic development as the foremost weapon for tackling terroristic activities. This area can be released from the clutches of terrorism only if the allegation of neglect and a change can be brought about in the behaviour of police-administration to the poor and indigent people. Because only transparent and dynamic administration can reduce the weight and appeal of the arguments of the Maoists. It is that path which Mamata Banerjee has adopted.

There can be no doubt that this will cause much uneasiness in the minds of the Maoists. As a result of identifying development and social justice as the guiding principles of the new government and as a result of opposition to CP(M) which is marked as the opponent party of the Maoists, the later have lost all the arguments against sitting in a conference with Mamata Banerjee. On the other hand the chief minister has shown administrative firmness against the demands of the Maoists for the removal of the CRP. She is firm in her resolution that the CRP will not be removed before the surrender of arms by the Maoists.

Under the circumstances the Maoists will have to ponder over the question why sitting in a conference is not the best solution for the sake of the greater interest of the poor people. Over and above that by giving the local people services in the police and by calling upon them to hold weapons in the interest of the country will undoubtedly put pressure on the Maoists.

In Bihar by way of allocating finance for the development of the Naxal-infested areas and bringing about development in the system of law and order Nitish Kumar obtained good dividends. His return in the election has been interpreted as an index of popular support to his policy of development. Therefore there is good likelihood that Mamata Banerjee also by way of bringing about development of education, health and nutrition will be able to check the advance of the Maoists and increase the support to her own party. Possibly this apprehension is at the root of the fact that the Maoists have prevented the villagers from attending the meetings of Mamata Banerjee. There is little doubt that Mamata Banerjee has succeeded in pressurising the Maoists and in this way given well-pronounced evidence of her political and administrative acumen.

3

STATE IS GOOD, MARKET EVIL

Market prices are rising in West Bengal and all the other regions of India and also China. The official authorities as well as the experts in Economics in different regions and different nations are anxious how the skyrocketing market prices can be brought under control. A certain and reliable remedy for controlling the prices has not been discovered by anybody in any country, otherwise prise-rise can never remain a nerve-racking problem-everybody from Wen Jia-Bao to Manmohan Singh would heave a sigh of relief. But an infallible remedy of this malady is ready at hand. It is a purely Bengali medicine made in Alimuddin Street.

A few days ago in a public meeting at Dharmatala the earlier chief minister Buddhadev Bhattacharya has proudly announced the secret of that medicine. He has declared that the commodities should be brought within the purview of the rationing system. The problem will be mitigated if the absolute necessaries like rice, pulses, wheat and oil can be sold at cheap prices through the fair price shops. But how the extra expenditure which are necessary for this purpose will be provided? Buddhadevbabu's easy prescription is that the government should give subsidies. It is from time immemorial that CP(M) had been distributing this good advice for public benefit but the national government has the incurable habit of paying no heed. The inevitable consequence is that the people had been burning at the fire of uncomfortable price-rise.

Before accusing Buddhadev Bhattacharya and his party let us consider another pertinent point. By defeating CP(M) powers have been captured by Trinamool Congress. The adverse attitude of the new chief minister Mamata Banerjee to Alimuddin is well known to everybody. But what about its principle and attitude to economic problems? Is Mamata Banerjee opposed to this principle? Let us make an analysis. No detailed analysis is necessary, an overall study is sufficient. As a result of the rise in price of diesel the cost of running the transport has increased. The regional government has announced that transport fares cannot be increased. Why? Because if transport fares are hiked the expenditures of the passengers will be increased. In other words the government's objective is to keep the fares at a low level. Whether the equilibrium between revenue and expenditure in the transport business is maintained as a consequence need not be taken into account.

It should be noticed that both the former chief minister and the present chief minister are unmindful of the market. Both of them believe in the principle of forcibly reducing the prices of rice, pulses, wheat and oil and the fares of buses, minibuses and taxis. Buddhadevbabu has in his speech indulged in the familiar Marxist condemnation of the market system. And his successor is attuning also her utterances easily with that strain.

It is unfortunate, but not strange. Whatever be the name of the party or whatever be the colour of the flag everybody in West Bengal is opposed to the market and is a votary of the control by the state.The leftist mind of this region is unwilling to subscribe to the primary principle of economics that the prices of goods and services in the market should be fixed in the open market by the free play of market forces of demand and supply. Hence the subsidisation of the prices of rice, pulses, wheat and oil and the fares of the buses, minibuses and taxis.If subsidies are not given what will happen to the poor?

The argument for giving subsidies to those who are truly poor is of course rational. But wholesale rationing or introduction of cheap fares at wholesale rates would only mean that the advantages will be mainly enjoyed by the middle class people in the short run. It is they who normally attend the meetings at Dharmatala, are passengers in the minibuses, are vocal, able and unified. And they also lack farsightedness. It is they who have ultimately to bear the brunt of the subsidies because these are provided finally from the public treasury.

But this is in fact a long-run affair. For the time being it is of course desirable that bus fares are kept at a low level and that food is available through fair price shops at subsidised rates. The whole thing is in fact the politics of appeasing the middle classes behind an ideal which is in favour of the control by the state and opposed to the operations of the market.

4

STRATEGY OF DEVELOPMENT - 2

A high level conference was held on June 15, 2011 at the Writer's Building with chief minister Mamata Banerjee for the purpose of discussing developmental activities at Jangalmahal. She has issued directions for making a package on an emergency basis for providing employment, supply of food and drinking water as well as medical services for the inhabitants of Jangalmahal. Among those who attended the meeting there were the chief secretary Samar Ghosh, Home Secretary GD Goutam and the Director General of Police Naparajit Mukherjee.

It has been decided that the government will take greater initiatives for giving to the young residents of Jangalmahal greater number of services in the police where at present there are quite a few thousands of vacant positions. The government is under the impression that by giving the young people of Jangalmahal services in the police the Maoist problem in the area can be mitigated. In case of necessity a seperate battalion of the police may be set up with the young people of Jangalmahal. In this way employment of the local people will ensure economic development of the area.

The chief minister previously declared that more people of Jangalmahal should be provided with rice at Rs. 2 per kg. She has issued direction to implement the project at a rapid pace. Her government has taken initiative so that in order that a single person in Jangalmahal does not remain in starvation rice should be provided free of cost. On this very day the chief minister visited the Food Department and issued instructions to the officers that rice and wheat should be distributed among the poor people before these are invaded by the insects.

The water Resources Development Department has already submitted a project of Rs. 22 crores for increasing the supply of drinking and irrigation water at Jangalmahal. Apart from accumulating ground water the Department has also emphasised the holding of rain water for this purpose.

The chief minister has also issued instructions to the Health Department so that satisfactory medical services are available at the health centres at Jangalmahal. The Health Department is giving special attention to the fact that there are no problems, relating to the availability of physicians and medicines in the health centres.

The chief minister has alerted all the departments to remain conscious so that the minimum requirements of living of the people of Jangalmahal do not remain unsatisfied.

5

FINANCE TANGLES

From the last month of May there was strong speculation that from the month of April, the government employees and the teachers will not receive their salaries. This was announced in different newspapers and TV channels and was discussed in the corridors of the government offices and even in the school and college compounds. Among the ministers also some were heard to express the apprehension of this financial crisis. And the then Finance Minister Asim Dasgupta had to visit New Delhi repeatedly in order to sit in conference with the Central Finance Minister Pranab Mukherjee so that a moribund regional economy can be kept enlivened for one or one and a half month till the election. Thereafter took place the popular mandate through the election of the Assembly. The disastrous defeat of the left front government after its continuous rule for thirty four years was followed by the installation of a new government under Trinmool Congress. This is the first time that after assuming the charge of ruling the region, the government received direct evidence of the fact of the bankruptcy of the treasury. Moreover, the predecessors have imposed upon the new government a huge burden of debt. Of course for the last few months the previous government had been repeatedly alerting the citizens of this region about this bankruptcy. This fact was also pointed out in their electoral manifesto and publicity campaign.

Under such critical conditions, the newly elected Finance Minister Amit Mitra was entrusted with the responsibility of managing the financial affairs of the regions. His ministerial career started through a serious crisis and the challenge to overcome it. No sooner than a single month was over, he had to submit the new budget. But this is not a full-fledged budget. In financial terms it is called 'Vote-on-Account Budget'.

It may be remembered in this context that since the election was due to be held in the month of May, the outgoing Finance Minister Asim Dasgupta also submitted a Vote-on-Account budget for the first four months of the new financial year (April 2011 - March 2012).

In fact, whenever a general election is held at the beginning of a financial year or whenever towards the end of a financial year, there occurs unexpectedly a natural or man-made disaster or, whenever due to some unavoidable reason there is not enough time for preparing a full-fledged budget a 'vote-on-account budget' is submitted. In case it is a regional budget, it has got to be submitted in the Legislative Assembly and recommended through a majority vote. If it is a central budget, it has to be passed in the Loksabha. The tenure of this budget is usually two months to six months.

Amit Mitra did not receive the minimum time of the few months necessary for preparing a full fledged budget. That apart he alleged that while submitting the vote-on-Account budget, his predecessor declared in the Annual Economic Report that the expected rate of increase of revenue will be 39 P.c. At the same time he showed the estimated amount of probable expenditure at a very low level. Amit Mitra complained that this statement was not only exaggerated, it was actually an unrealistic myth. And the ordinary citizens of the region have in this way been deliberately confused. This was another reason why he had to submit a fresh 'Vote-on-Account Budget.'

Amit Mitra has submitted a budget for two months only August and September. The allotment is to the extent of Rs. 11,165 crores 62 lakhs 22 thousand only. The subjects to which has been paid special notice and additional importance are rural health and drinking water project, universal education or secondary education and the midday meal project, constitution of 17 clusters of small and medium industries (and additional job creation through this process), development of Jangalmahal, Sunderban and development of hill areas etc.

In short, emphasis has been laid on the development of social and physical infrastructures, development of human resources and development of the neglected backward areas of the region. These matters were given importance in the pre-electoral publicity campaigns as well as the manifesto of Trinamool Congress. It is remarkable that although the 'Vote-on-Account' is only a temporary and partial budget the Finance Minister has remembered their earlier promises to the people.

For the purpose of getting the necessary finance to this end, he has to put greatest reliance on grants from the central government. Already along with the Chief Minister, he has attended fruitful conferences with the central Finance Minister, Prime Minister and the Deputy Chairman of the Planning Commission.

Apart from relying on grants from the centre Mr. Mitra has also mentioned the need for making wholehearted efforts by the region for boosting the total internal production. If this can be successfully materialised in the short run, the credibility of the regional government will be enhanced.

The disappointing circumstances which are created in both the fields of internal production and revenue collection during the years of the last leftist regime were responsible for the questionable credibility of the region. In the recent years Reserve Bank of India alerted many times the erstwhile government on account of the financial distress of the region and also for taking too much credit in overdraft. There are instances of meeting official expenditures by taking credit from DFID which is an organisation under the British government.

The upper limit of the credit to be received from the centre in the present financial year was Rs. 17,800 crores. From this amount Rs. 5,000 crores are withdrawn in the last two months before the election by the leftist government. The new government after installation in power has withdrawn another Rs. 3,000 crores of rupees as emergency credit with a view to paying the salaries of the government employees and the teachers and also meeting the routine expenses of paying the pensions of the retired people and the widow allowances. Because it has inherited from the last government an empty treasury. Therefore almost half the amount of the total credit limit has already been withdrawn within three months of the current financial year While mentioning this pathetic situation Amit Mitra has also alerted that the burden of debt of this region is 2 lakh 3 thousand 867 crores of rupees or, in other words our per capita credit is 22 thousand 638 crores of rupees at the present moment.

But following the FRBM Act, West Bengal government could much earlier put a check on financial indiscipline. In that case the region could be saved from the current debacle. In fact with the exception of Sikkim, West Bengal is the only region within the nation which defied this Act and did not implement it till the middle of 2010.

It was argued then that in case of implementation of this law, the expenditure for various activities in the social sphere as well as many public welfare activities have to be severely curtailed. The real truth, however, was that in the garb of this rationale indulgence was being given to many kinds of financial irregularities which had been continuing for a pretty long time.

As per the FRBM Act, the deficit in different accounts of the government are to be regularly reduced at predetermined rates, the amounts of credit from the Reserve Bank as well as the open market are to be restricted and transparency was to be maintained in the official financial matters. From the information received from RBI, it is learnt that West Bengal happens to be one of those regions where the proportion of credit in relation to the total internal production were highest. This proportion was 47.0% on an average in 2005-08 and the positions of Bihar and Uttar Pradesh were very near this figure. In the year 2008-09 this figure was reduced somewhat to 42.5%. But in that year all the other regions except U.P. improved their circumstances from good to better conditions. Even Bihar also registered much improvement in their unenviable circumstances and reached a higher position. But West Bengal was a failure. It does not appear that the other regions incurred any loss by following the FRBM Act.

Amit Mitra has observed that this year's Annual Economic Report was based on the CAG calculations for 2010-11 and not on the basis of fictitious statistics.

It has already been mentioned that the 'vote-on-Account Budget' is not a detailed full-fledged budget. This is merely a short-term makeshift budget. In this budget only the broad outlines of the allotments are given. Unlike the Interim Budget the detailed sources of income or the accounts of both revenue and expenditure are not required to be presented. Because very often this budget is prepared within a short period for short term purposes. Apart from that it is the headache of the new government to determine how financing for two or four months will be carried out. That is why 'Vote on Account Budget' is usually passed without any detailed debates. And whenever it is submitted by a new government, it is expected that the opposition will normally consider it with democratic decency.

Nonetheless the opposition leader was very vocal about why the sources of revenue were not mentioned in detail in Amit Mitra's budget. This fact was also mentioned at large in their party organ. Aspersions have also been made over the pronunciation difficulties of the Finance Minister during his budget speech. All this indicates the lack of courtesy of the oppositionists in the Assembly.

But more discourteous and contrary to democratic ideas was the empty treasury left for the successor by the previous Finance Minister and the huge burden of debt.

Because the chief ideal of democracy is to give due respect as well as ample facilities to the opposition, it is regrettable that Amit Mitra did not receive this facility although their government is in its infancy now and they have now 'many miles to go' in the matter of administration.

It is not improper to raise the question why despite 35 years' continuous dominance the leftist government failed to build up a strong and stable economy. Why the previous Finance Minister after staying in the government at a stretch for twenty years made the regional economy sick and bankrupt although he gave for many years the stunt of a Zero-deficit budget and an alternative development model. Will they even now accuse for this failure 'the deprivation by the Centre', 'limited power of the region' and 'the problem of globalisation'?

6

DEVELOPMENT IN COUNTRY-SIDE

The regional government is making due arrangements for the rehabilitation of those inhabitants of Marichjhampi who espcaped to save their lives from the carnage committed by the onslaught of the police as well as the militant activists of the Communist Party of India (Marxist). That attempt has started under the initiative of the Refugee Rehabilitation Department. The work of registering the names of the previous residents of Marichjhampi has been going on in the Kareya area in Barasat since 30th June, 2011. About one and a half year ago, the refugees of Marichjhampi themselves set up an organisation. It is that organisation which has started the work of identifying the earlier residents of Marichjhampi. They are desirous of rehabilitation in Marichjhampi once again. The members of the organization have already met the Chief Minister Mamata Banerjee and apprised her of their problems. The organisation informed that apart from rehabilitation the Chief Minister has also given the assurance of an inquiry into the entire Marichjhampi episode.

The Minister of state of the Refugee Rehabilitation Department, Manjul Krishna Thakur has wanted a list of names of the victims from them. As soon as the names are registered that list will be handed over to the Minister. It is a lamented fact that after the Marichjhampi massacre, many refugees were displaced from their original habitat. Although the government of Jyoti Basu sent them back once again to Dandakaranya, many of them went underground in this very region. Presently they are living in different regions of India. Till now they have no lands of their own. The leftist government paid no heed to any of their appeals. On the contrary they were given the threat to send them back to Dandakaranya.

Quite a few thousands of refugees of Marichjhampi are living in Barasat, Deganga, Madhyamgram, Gobardanga, Gosaba, Kumirmari and Ranaghat. Although many refugees of Bangladesh received rehabilitation in West Bengal, the refugees of Marichjhampi were so unfortunate that they received nothing other than deprivation.

Manjul Krishna Babu informed that he had discussed this problem with the Chief Minister who was highly sincere in the matter of solving this problem. Adequate arrangements of rehabilitation of these hapless people will be undertaken. A form has already been prepared on behalf of the Refugee Rehabilitation Committee in which the names of all the members of the families, their present addresses and the respective experiences of the victims of the Marichjhampi episode will be included.

The Chief Minister Mamata Banerjee is well aware that the solution of the Jangalmahal problem is a big challenge to her government. Even before the election Mamata has repeatedly asserted that if they ever come to power they will leave no stones unturned in solving the Jangalmahal problem. Her government will pay adequate attention to the all sided development of Jangalmahal which is totally deprived from the light of development. Utmost importance has been laid on the problem of lack of development in the electoral manifesto of the Trinamool Congress.

Mamata Banerjee did not ultimately forget her electoral assurances. The very next day of assuming the changes of the Chief Minister, she started discussions in different circles regarding her duties in respect of the indigent people of Jangalmahal. On Sunday Mamata declared that the district magistrates and the district Superintendents of police should act with wartime alacrity so that each of the poor persons in Jangalmahal can get at least two square meals a day. Without caring for governmental formalities of redtapism, the new Chief Minister has issued directives to the district magistrates and district superintendents of police to provide food for the starving people in the first instance and think of the official formalities thereafter. In other words, the Chief Minister has asked her subordinates to see to it that bureaucratic bunglings are avoided so that food reaches the hungry people without delay.

Following the directives of the Chief Minister the Food Minister

Jyotipriya Mallik is going very soon to visit West Medinipur. Before that he has already informed that the regional government will start a 'Food for all' programme in order to reach food for each of the indigent persons of Jangalmahal. In case any family remains hungry and that information reaches the administration, reasures should be adopted to reach rice to that family within two hours. The additional expenses incurred for this purpose should be subsidised from the Food Department.

It is all too evident that through all these declarations, the Chief Minister is trying to present a human face of her administration. And she is careful that this human face does not obliterate as a result of any bureaucratic complexity. That is why, sidetracking many unnecessary bureaucratic restrictions, she is talking of putting emphasis on public interest. This attitude and initiative of the Chief Minister are welcome for many reasons. So long the bureaucratic complexties were given undue importance. It is a fact that questions of public interest have very often been neglected as a result of redtapism and governmental indifference.

These bureaucratic mindset and the official indifference were responsible for the most part for the lack of development in this long period after the independence. During the previous left front government five bureacrats were sent to Jangalmahal by a helicopter. Returning from that place, they submitted a few proposals regarding the development of Jangalmahal to the regional government. But as a result of the bureaucratic complexities none of those proposals were ultimately implemented. It is really thanksworthy that the new Chief Minister by demolishing that obsolete structure is laying stress on the building of a humane administration.

But, at the same time one important matter should be kept in mind. In order to remove the poverty of Jangalmahal a correct blueprint for the development of this area has to be drawn up. This problem cannot be solved only by distributing rice through subsidies through the rationing system. If the whole system becomes solely dependent on subsidies, the government will itself find it difficult to continue the system for long. It is well and good that the government is arranging to supply rice at Rs. 2 per kg to the starving people. But at the same time, it should adopt arrangements so that all the inhabitants of that area can receive work throughout the entire year. Adequate planning has to be undertaken by the government for this purpose. Mamata Banerjee has already announced that all the young men of this area will be given employment in the police force.

The handicrafts of the Adivasis of Jangalmahal should be placed in the world market by numerous little self-help groups and their income opportunities should be ensured in this way. The forest areas of Jangalmahal should be utilised for the purpose of expansion of the tourism industry. The government will have to frame plans so that the income opportunities of the local people can expand depending on the tourism industry. By means of utilising in a befitting manner, the forest areas of Jangalmahal in the field of herbal treatment income opportunties of the local residents may be further expanded.

For the conservation of rain water and ground water for drinking purposes, adequate arrangements have to be made. Apart from drinking water medical treatment and education should be made available to the deprived people of Jangalmahal. In other words, the government must of necessity cultivate a far-reaching outlook beside which they must posses a sincere political will to work for the common masses. Only a little ray of development is sufficient to enlighten the entire area of Jangalmahal.

Just where the shoe pinches in Jangalmahal is nothing new to Mamata Banerjee. At least two decades ago she witnessed with her own eyes how the people of Jangalmahal pass their days. If in the light of that experience, she now wisely draws up a blueprint for the development of the area the local people will reap ample dividends.

7

MORE ABOUT JANGALMAHAL

The Chief Minister Mamata Banerjee has taken initiatives for a political solution of the Jangalmahal tangle. Very recently the bigwigs of her government met the representatives of the civil society in a long conference at the end of which the Chief Minister apprised that she was determined to establish peace in Jangalmahal at any cost. She also informed that very soon she would visit the area with a special package of economic and social development. At the same time the Chief Minister has also appealed to the Maoists to hold their weapons. She has assured them that the Allied Forces will be withdrawn from Jangalmahal on the return of peace.

Without naming the Maoists she has assured them that the government is willing to sit in conference with them over the return of peace, in Jangalmahal. In order to create suitable atmosphere for that meeting, she has also entrusted a few representatives of the civil society with that responsibility. This interest of the Chief Minister for solving the Jangalmahal problem through discussion in this way has only expressed the sincerity of the new government.

The difference between this initiative of the new government with the line of action of the previous government is that the previous government showed no interest at all in the creation of a suitable climate for mutual discussion. On the contrary the previous government chose the path of state-controlled violence and oppression. The left front government failed to realise that police atrocities can never suppress totally the movement which broke out as a reaction against deprivation and lack of development. They also failed to understand that perhaps police action can temporarily suppress a mass movement but the grievances of the people still did not vanish. Rather

8

NEW ERA IN THE HILLS

The residents of the Hills have marked the day July 18, 2011 as a historic day. In all the senses the day is really historic. With a view to restoring peace in the Hills the Gorkha Territorial Administration Treaty has been signed on this day at the initiatives of the national Home Minister Palaniappan Chidambaram and the regional chief minister Mamata Banerjee. A new era has started in the Hills. The residents of the Hills have also been overwhelmed with joy at this Treaty. They have got the impression that many of their demands have been considered by the chief minister of the new government with adequate sympathy. The ovations of the residents of the Hills have almost overflooded the chief minister. After taking oath as the chief minister Mamata Banerjee declared that establishment of peace in the Hills is her immediate objective. She also gave the assurance that within one hundred days she will perform this task. Looked at from that point of view she has progressed a lot towards the objective of establishing peace much before the scheduled time limit of one hundred days.

Previously on August 22,1982 a treaty was signed about the Hills in the Rajbhavan. By virtue of that treaty the Darjeeling Gorkha Hill Council was constituted. Subas Ghishing signed in that treaty in the presence of the then chief minister Jyoti Basu and the national Home Minister Buta Singh. The difference between the present treaty and the earlier one is that the Gorkhaland Territorial Administration received more than before. Previously the representation of the government in the Hill Council was much greater. Among the total number of 42 members, 14 were the re-presentatives of the government. This time the representation of the government is much less. Among a total number of 50 members only five are the representatives of the government. Apart from that this time there are many more departments in the hands of the Gorkhaland Territorial Administration, the power of liberally using the finances of the national and regional governments remaining in its hands, in comparison to the Gorkha Hill Council the number of seats has increased much in the Territorial Administration. What is most important is that a probable road remains open of the probability to bring some portion of Terai and Dooars within the jurisdiction of the Territorial Administration.

After receiving all these concessions from the new government the chief of the Gorkha Janamukti Morcha Bimal Gurung and his followers are naturally quite happy. It can reasonably be expected that after the signing of the treaty they will give up their earlier demands for a separate Gorkhaland and pay greater attention to the development of the Hills and cooperate with the government by all means to establish peace and harmony in the Hills.

Both the national Home Minister Chidambaram and the regional chief minister made it clear on the day of signing the treaty that both of them are sincere on the question of development of the Hills. And this is the reason why they have handed over greater powers to the new Territorial Administration. But they have also made it clear that they are not supporting the demand for a seperate Gorkhaland and that Darjeeling should not be isolated from West Bengal.

In his speech Chidambaram emphasised that India is unity in diversity. The area whose responsibility is being handed over to the Territorial Administration consists of many religions, castes, languages and cultures. The Territorial Administration must remain equally respectful to everybody. And the chief minister Mamata Banerjee has spoken in more clearcut terms that Darjeeling is not outside West Bengal which is not going to be divided. The leaders of the Gorkha Janamukti Morcha will have to understand the import of the speeches of the home minister and the chief minister. Bimal Gurung and all the other leaders of the Gorkha Janamukti Morcha must be careful so that they never have to face the allegation of breach of trust against the home minister and the chief minister.

All the parties involved must concern themselves with the question of establishing peace in the Hills and expedite the process of development of these areas. During the eighties the Hills have burnt for long in the fire of unrest. Of course, after the signing of Gorkha Hill Council Treaty in 1988 the Hills were peaceful for quite some time. But that peace was of a very short duration. As a result of the movement of the Gorkha Janamukti Morcha and the driving away of Ghishing, the Hills became heated once again. This unrest has repeatedly provoked disorder in the public life of the Hills.

The tourism industry of the Hills on which most of the local residents are dependent have suffered severely. Other lines of trade and Commerce in the Hills were also not exempted. As a whole the path of progress in the Hills was blocked. Repetition of turmoil in the Hills cannot be desirable. It is urgently necessary to evolve a durable solution of the problems of the Hills. It is now desirable that through the constitution of the new Territorial Administration a durable solution of the Hills problem must be enacted and the Hills will once again return to their natural rhythm.

Every year the national government will grant the new Territorial Administration an amount of Rs. 200 crores. This financial year help will continue for the first three years after the constitution of the autonomous Administration.

The responsibility of those who are being empowered with this objective in view is the greatest. They will have to remember that the power which is vested in them must be *Properly* utilised. They must have a steadfast attitude towards the development of the Hills. They will have to remember that their commitments to the people of all religions and all cultures living in the Hills are equal. And above all they must be in a position to appreciate the truth that the Hills are an inalienable part of West Bengal, not a seperate territory outside the borders of the region.

9

AGONY OF AGRICULTURE

The initiative that the new government of West Bengal has adopted with a view to returning the lands of the unwilling peasants at Singur has recently fallen in a much more complex vortex. On June 28, 2011 as a result of the efforts of the Chief Minister Mamata Banerjee the administration started the work of returning the lands of the unwilling peasants. In the evening on that day 12 peasants were shown the plots of land fixed for them. It was decided that in the morning on the very next day the papers relating to the ownership of those lands will be handed over to them. But on the previous day the Tatas appealed to the Supreme Court for an injunction over the land distribution process at Singur. Consequently, owing to the complexities of the legal system, the whole process has become more complicated. It is not clear even now how this tie of complication will be simplified. What is explicit is that the Tatas will not very easily agree to give up the ownership of the land at Singur.

In such a perspective the Chief Minister Mamata Banerjee has also advanced an important demand. She has claimed that in all those places throughout the country where land has been acquired in the name of building up industries but left unutilised such lands should be immediately returned to the original owners. In this context she has pleaded for returning the land by amending the Act of 1894.

A little observation will indicate that as things stand today in different corners of the country, unrest has been intensified around the question of land acquisition. Direct conflicts have broken out between the regional governments on the one hand and those peasants and sons of the soil who have lost their lands on the other. It is not unoften that these conflicts are causing much bloodshed and loss of lives. Nor are such land skirmishes confined to Singur alone. Land movement has now broken out in various important places in the political landscape. In the Jagatsinghpur district in Orissa, a conflict is going on between the Orissa government and the sons of the soil over land acquisition for the proposed Poscoe factory. The residents of Jagatsinghpur has come down to the streets to build up direct resistance movement against land acquisition. In the Greater Noida area of Uttar Pradesh the local peasants have built up mass movement in protest against urbanisation by means of acquisition of fertile agricultural lands. This movement has become the headache of the Supreme Court who has observed that they do not want the happening of another Nandigram. It has also alerted the U.P. Government that in case of necessity it is prepared to intervene in the matter. The peasants movement in Singur and the effort of the new government in the following period to return the lands of the peasants by way of legislation- all these will leave their impact on the land movements elsewhere. It goes without saying that Singur will become the model in land movements throughout the nation.

Under the circumstances the national government will have to consider the matter with great importance. In the first place the government will have to realise that the Land Acquisition Act which was passed by the British government in 1894 cannot remain in force even to this day. Following the demands of time and circumstances this law should have been amended much earlier which however, the government failed to do. Of course, the national government is now saying that this law will be amended in the coming session of the Loksabha. Right now the government should start speculation regarding how lands should be returned to the peasants by amending this law. What the Chief Minister Mamata Banerjee opined in this matter is appropriate.

At the time of amending this law, the government should keep in mind one important matter. It is that a law is enacted chiefly with the purpose of safeguarding the interests of the citizens. If ever by evading the restrictions imposed by the law anybody wants to hurt the interest of the citizens, it is the government's duty to resist such misconceived attempts. That is why the Act of 1894 should be amended in such wise that everywhere the interests of the sons of the soil are safeguarded. Constant vigil should be maintained so that the sons of the soil are not deprived of, their natural rights are not downtrodden and any land shark cannot receive the opportunity to engulf the lands of any poor peasant. A piece of land not only ensures the life and livelihood of a peasant family throughout generations, but also it becomes the determinant of the social identity of a son of the soil. The government will have to understand in the light of sociology the probable impact on the society if this condition is destroyed. The more delay is done by the government in this matter the feeling of deprivation in the minds of the sons of soil will become greater and greater. The feeling of grievance will continue to simmer in the public psyche in different corners and that is why the government should take adequate steps before that fire engulfs the entire social superstructure.

10

TURMOIL OVER ACQUISITION

The vitriolic comment which the Supreme Court recently passed in connexion with a case relating to land acquisition while rebuking the Mayabati government in Uttar Pradesh is considerably significant in the contemporary perspective. Supreme Court has commented that taking advantage of a colonial law, the poor people's lands are snatched away from their hands in order to build up shopping malls and residential complexes. In this way ordinary people are being marginalised in the name of 'globalisation'. Numerous incidents of suicide which are taking place as a result have only one reason at their roots. People are gradually being sent to the end of a precipice.

However, at the same time on the same day in the Kolkata city the new Chief Minister of West Bengal Mamata Banerjee has adopted a few important decisions regarding the landed properties of the rural peasants. The Chief Minister has decided that her government will not apply special powers in the case of acquisition of land. Even if a single square yard of land is to be acquired, the concerned department will have to submit a proposal to that effect to the Ministry. The Ministry will adopt a decision only after considering such questions as to why the land is required, how much land is required, what is the character of land and what are the likely social consequences of the acquisition.

A little speculation will reveal that there is a close nexus between the verdict of the Supreme Court and the decision of Mamata Banerjee. The thought processes of both the parties are flowing along the same channel.

There is little gain in denying the fact that during the last few years, there has appeared unrest in different corners of the nation over the land acquisition question. Everywhere there is the allegation against the regional government over the issue of acquisition of land of the poor villagers. There is the allegation that taking advantage of the Land Acquisition Act of 1894 and in the interest of multinational industrial organisations attempts are going on in different regions to capture the lands of the poor people. Nor can it be asserted that such allegations are totally fabricated. It is over the question of forcible land acquisition that the grievances of the rural masses against the leftist government were crystallised as a consequence of which the left front had to bid adieu from power. It can not also be denied that the lands of the poor masses were snatched away for building the luxury palaces of the upper classes." At least Rajarhat is an instance of this occurrence in our region. The land movement is now gradually gathering momentum and assuming the form of a main stream movement. Already the demand for amending the Land Acquisition Act of 1894 has been advanced. The national government is also now thinking about amending this law in the coming session of the Parliament.

The Supreme Court is now realizing that the land movement is gradually becoming more and more violent in the countryside and ordinary people are being exploited by taking resort to the colonial law of 1894. Because also in the past in this case relating to land acquisition in Uttar Pradesh, Supreme Court issued a warning that another Nandigram was not necessary. And this time the appeal of the U.P. government has been rejected by the Supreme Court.

It is as a result of movement against the forcible acquisition of land that the present Chief Minister Mamata Banerjee has come to power. She is well aware that a piece of land does not ensure only economic security but it also indicates a person's proper identity in the social-political milieu or social ambience. Mamata understands well the agonies of the landless persons and that is why she is eager to avoid the mistaken steps of the earlier government in the case of land acquisition. She has already issued a directive that so long as an account of the unutilized land in the hands of the government is not prepared, no further acquisition will take place. At the same time the Chief Minister has also emphasised in detail the necessity of examining in advance the possible social impact of such forcible acquisition.

Neither in the case of Singur or Nandigram this social impact was kept in mind by the previous government and they had also to suffer the inevitable consequences on this account.

Two honourable judges of the Supreme Court G.S. Singhbhi and Ashoke Gangopadhyaya rebuked the U.P. Government in the following terms: 'Do you think that we the judges live in a 'paradise of fools'? By way of misusing a largely outdated colonial law, you are jeopardising the interests of the ordinary citizens, If those two judges knew that on that very day the Chief Minister of West Bengal has adopted this populist and responsible decision, they would certainly have eulogised her abundantly. Perhaps they would have advised other regions to follow the West Bengal model. The honourable judges of the Supreme Court would very certainly remind the governments of all the other regions to learn from Mamata Banerjee that it is the government which is entrusted with the duty of protecting the fundamental rights of the umpteen millions of the nation as well as the respective regions.

11

RETURNING LANDS OF UNWILLING PEASANTS

The intiative taken by the new Government to return the lands of the unwilling peasants at Singur was stumbled on 29th June, 2011. On the previous day as a result of the efforts of the Chief Minister Mamata Banerjee the administration started the work of returning the lands of the unwilling peasants. In the evening of that day 12 peasants were shown the plots of land specified for them. It was decided that in the morning on the next day the documents regarding the ownership of those plots of lands would be transferred to their hands. But on Tuesday, i.e., the previous day, the TATAs approached the Supreme Court with an appeal for the stay order on the land allotment process. On next day morning the Supreme Court issued an injunction in the perspective of this appeal of the TATAs. Consequently as a result of the legal complexities the whole process has became complicated. It is not clear when these complications will become simplified. What is obvious is that the TATAs will not easily agree to give up the ownership of the land at Singur. In these circumstances the Chief Minister Mamata Banerjee has advanced an important claim. She has demanded that wherever land has been acquired in the name of industry and development throughout the regions and kept unutilised should be returned forthwith to the original owners. In this context she pleaded for amending the Land Acquisition Act of 1894 and returning the lands without delay.

A little scrutiny will reveal that unrest has appeared in different corners of the country over the question of acquisition. Landless peasants and sons of the soil are coming in direct conflict with the regional governments. Occasionally these conflicts are assuming the appearances of bloody carnages. Nor is this land movement confined to Singur alone the land movement has appeared in important hotbeds in the political map throughout the length and breadth of the entire nation. In the Jagatsingpur District of Orissa a conflict is going on between the Orissa Government and the sons of the soil over the issue of the acquisition of land for the proposed Poscoe factory. The residents of Jagatsingpur have come down to the streets and directly built up mass resistance against the government. In Greater Noida of Uttar Pradesh the local peasants have waged up movements in protest against urbanisation through the acquisition of fertile agricultural lands. This movement has provoked the Supreme Court in arguing that they are not interested in witnessing another Nandigram carnage. It has also alerted the U.P. Government that it will intervene in these matters if need be. The peasant's movement in Singur and the effort to return the lands of the peasants by enacting law by the new government in the following period will also cast their shadow on land movements elsewhere. It can be safely asserted that Singur will this time become the model in the matter of land movement throughout the entire nation.

Under these circumstances the national government will like to attach adequate importance to this matter. In the first place it has got to be understood that the Land Acquisition Act (1894) of the British Government can no longer be valid under the present circumstances. This law should have been amended much earlier as per the requirements of the time and the circumstances. The government however failed to do that. Although the national government is now giving the assurance that in the coming session of the Loksabha the law will be amended. The Government will have to immediately start speculation as to how the law may be amended and the lands may be returned to the dispossessed peasants.

While amending this law the Government will have to remember another matter. It is that law is enacted principally with the purpose of protecting the interests of the citizens. If any power bypasses that law and attaches the interest of the citizens of the nations the Government should come forward to resist that power. That is why the Act of 1894 should be amended in such a way that the rights of the sons of the soil are protected everywhere. It should be ensured that the sons of the soil are not deprived of their natural rights and the landowners are not enabled to grab the lands of peasants with the assistance or connivance of law. A piece of land not only ensures the life and livelihood of a peasant family through generations, it also becomes the determinant of the social identity of a peasant family who are the children of the soil. The Government has to perceive in the light of sociology the impact of this iedntity in the society. If the government makes undue delay in understanding this simple truth the sons of the soil will suffer from greater feeling of exploitation and deprivation. The fire of grievance will engulf the entire countryside. The government should therefore remain alert on this account.

12

SINGUR ORDINANCE

The regional government has recently imposed an Ordinance to return to the peasants the lands forcibly acquired for the purpose of building an automobile factory at Singur. Many debates and controversies may appear on this score. Particularly CPI(M) has already declared this step as unconstitutional. Their upshot is that when the Assembly is continuing this sort of Ordinance which bypasses it is equivalent to violating the constitution. But the whip of that party in the Assembly Rejjak Molla has made no bones about welcoming this decision of the Chief Minister, Mamata Banerjee. No wonder that this sudden decision of the new government has confounded the CPM. This is obvious from the internal dissension of the party.

Through this Ordinance, within 21 days of coming into power, Mamata Banerjee lived upto the number one electoral assurance of Trinamools Congress. Her victory started from the very first day of embarking in the movement against the snatching away of the lands of the peasants of Singur. From the very first day that it was known that she has stood by the side of the poor, downtrodden peasants in the rural areas of Bengal, CPM has become paralysed. In all the elections in Panchayat, Loksabha and Vidhansabha Mamata Banerjee gave the assurance of remaining by the side of the poor and indigent people of rural Bengal and the highest priority was laid during the Assembly election on returning the lands to the peasants of Singur. This Ordinance of the new government is an indication that those assurances were not mere eyewash is also clear from this Ordinance. If the assurance to return the lands to the peasants was a mere eyewash the government could take time in an unjustified manner by giving excuse of the legislation of the British period. Because the Land Acquisition Act of 1894 could not be easily amended for the asking of the government. Much efforts would have been required for that purpose. Other regions of the Indian nation have also to suffer on account of the British Land Act because the legal complications are extremely complex. If Mamata believed that the assurances given in the manifesto were merely a few electoral stunts she could very easily sidetrack the issue. But she did not do that. Rather with the understanding that much time will be required for amending the law, she has rapidly declared the Ordinance in order that the peasants are not deprived. In other words she has given a definite proof of the proposition that where there is a will there is a way. Perhaps this particular measure of the West Bengal government will show the other regions the necessary direction for solving their respective problems.

When the Tatas took the decision to shift their operations from Singur to Gujarat as a result of the dharna movement of the local peasants under the leadership of Mamata Banerjee, the then ruling party CPI(M) and the so called votaries of industrialisation began to cry wolf. The question that they raised was what will be the next happenings. Now that the Tatas have left West Bengal industry will in this region go to rack and ruin. The hopes of the peasants that they will get back their lands are unfounded. They will never receive back the lands which they have already lost. Such happenings are impossible under the present legal system. And for all these debacles is responsible the obstincy of Mamata Banerjee.

But today after the declaration of this Ordinance CPI(M) has realised that no such comments can be made. It has therefore only raised questions about the constitutional legitimacy of the Ordinance. But the thing to regret is that in this case also there is lack of understanding in the midst of the opposition. That is why on behalf of the party Suryakanta Misra is saying one thing while the ex-Land and Land Reform Minister Rejjak Molla who calls himself a 'peasant's son' is arguing in a different channel. The latter has openly supported this measure of the new government. What, now, will be the course of action of the legislators of CPI(M) in the opposition bench when the Chief Minister-cum-Land Minister Mamata Banerjee will submit the bill in the House during the next Assembly Election? Will they attune their utterings to the opposition leader or will they welcome the decision of the Chief Minister by following the instance of the whip of the party ?

Controversy over this Ordinance is not unlikely. Nonetheless the peasant community of not only Singur but also the entire rural Bengal is delighted at this instance of taking bold steps and rapid decisions of Mamata Banerjee i.e. the Alliance government by taking into consideration the happiness or otherwise of the peasant community. Time was when the peasant community of undivided Bengal regarded Fazlul Haqtue as a person of their own. The down-to-earth politics of Fazlul Haque kindled among them new hopes of living. When the left government was installed in power in 1977 the poverty-stricken agriculturists wrongly presupposed that their happy days have returned once again. But there was little delay in belying their hopes. It was the party leaders who were responsible for exploiting this expectation of theirs. Probably the Singur Ordinance will raise new hopes in the minds of the peasants. We can only expect that Mamata Banerjee's new government will attach due importance to this optimism.

13

CONFISCATING LANDS OF TATAS

Many leftist leaders and activists have been started at the way the Chief Minister Mamata Banerjee has confiscated the lands of the Tata Project at Singur by declaring an Ordinance. Although a few leaders of CP(M) have opposed the Ordinance by raising a few technical questions, many leftwing people have welcomed the decision of Mamata Banerjee. They cherish the impression that there is no precedent in our country of the vehement struggle that the Trinamool supremo has waged for the last five years against a big industrial organisation like the Tatas. It is doubtful whether any other regional government or even the powerful national government could show the courage to deliver such a big blow to a mighty organization like the TATAs.

It was in 1968 that the youth wing of CPI(M) DYF held a convention in Howrah. In that convention not unlike the other Marxists the regional Secretary of DYF Buddhadeva Bhattacharya raised the battle cry of confiscating the properties of Tatas and Birlas. There was a time when all the communists of this country always used to mouth the slogans of confiscating the properties of the capitalists like the Tatas and Birlas. But in the long run they have all detracted from their earlier paths. To speak the truth, Buddhadeva Bhattacharya has undergone a somersault. During the last five years in his capacity as the Chief Minister he has been converted into a lackey of the Tatas and the Birlas. His government has handed over lands worth crores of rupees to the Tatas and Birlas.

For example, in order to acquire the land at Singur at least 150 crores of rupees were spent from the public exchequer. Tatas were given lease of 600 acres of land on such easy terms that in five years the government earnings will amount to only 5 crores of rupees. If the land was given lease by following proper regulations, the Tatas would have to pay at least Rs. 100 crores in the very first year. Apart from that the huge advantages which the left front government gave to the Tatas ensure that the Nano cars would be manufactured in West Bengal at government expenses.

The left front government has given away lands for long not only to the Tatas but also to the Birlas, Batas and Salims. All the necessary regulations were bypassed and in the name of renovation of the factory, they gave the permission for selling surplus land to the extent of 314 acres to the Hind Motor Factory of the Birlas in Uttarpara, Hooghly. That land was transferred to the Hind Motor authorities in exchange for only Rs. 10 crores. It was argued that Rs. 84 crores which will be obtained by selling the land will be spent for the purpose of renovating the factory. Ultimately it was known that by selling the land, the Hind Motor authorities have amassed Rs. 284 crores.

The same thing has happened in the case of Bata in South 24 Parganas. In this case also the surplus 262 acres of land of the factory were handed over by the left front government to the Bata company in exchange for Rs. 12 crores only. There also the owner of the land was the government. In both the two areas of Hind Motor and Bata it was proposed that townships, shopping malls, schools and hospitals for the rich should be built up. The land scandal of Bidhannagar is under the consideration of the industrial Committee. On the other hand much turmoil is going on in Bata over this issue for long.

No less obeisance was paid by Buddhadeva Bhattacharya and Nirupam Sen to the Salims. They handed over the Nayachar island of 45 square kilometers in exchange for Rs. 25 crores only to Salim and his company, for the purpose of building a chemical hub. As per the opinion of the Land Department of the region the market price of that land is Rs. 1268 crores only. The new government should scrutinise whether anybody's personal interest is hidden behind these land deals. At the same time all these lands should be confiscated and taken into the custody of the governments

Owing to the scarcity of land the housing projects of the poor people like Indira Abasan Prakalpa and Ambedkar Yojana are suffering. Crores of rupees granted by the national government are being returned. It is the duty of the new government to confiscate these land deals and scrutinise all the relevant matters. If land has to be allotted such conditions should be imposed that ensure the construction of residential complexes, schools, colleges and hospitals principally for the benefit of the poor for the simple reason that it is the poor and weaker section of the people from whom this government receives its principal support.

14

VICTORY OF THE PEASANTS

The movement for preserving the agricultural lands in Singur gave political reestablishment to the Trinamool Congress supremo Mamata Banerjee. Following the disaster in the Assembly election of 2006 when everybody had the impression that the political future of Mamata Banerjee was totally bleak, right at that moment the movements of Singur and Nandigram supplied oxygen to Trinamool Congress. The strength of that movement was so great that within five years Mamata tornado totally destroyed the last remnants of CPI(M). The political pundits had dubious ideas regarding the political future of Mamata Banerjee in 2006 but in 2011, she has been installed in the position of the Chief Minister of West Bengal. The Singur episode which gave her the opportunity to turn around once again in politics was not forgotten by Mamata Banerjee. Even before the election she has repeatedly asserted that if she is returned to power, she will definitely return the lands of the unwilling peasants of Singur. On the twenty fourth day of being returned to power with the objective of returning the lands of the unwilling peasants of Singur on June 14, 2011 she passed the historic. 'Singur Land Rehabilitation and Development Bill 2011.' In a sense on this day the Chief Minister of the new government gave official recognition to the landless peasants of Singur and their demands.

It was as a consequence of going to acquire agricultural lands by brute force that the previous leftist government ensured their own downfall. Following the Singur episode the peasant community of rural Bengal turned away their face from the leftist government. The Singur episode made it as clear as daylight that instead of safeguarding the interest of the peasants, the government of Buddhadeva Bhattacharya was more interested in protecting the interests of the big capitalists and industrialists. Of course, the highest leaders of CPI(M) are now admitting that the Singur and Nandigram episodes use at the root of the fall of the leftist government. In the recently held Central Committee Conference of CPI(M) in Hyderabad, the all-India General Secretary of CPI(M) Prakash Karat has also confessed that it had been highly improper to acquire lands in Singur and Nandigram in a forcible manner. Much earlier, the Singur and Nandigram incidents snatched away the earth from under the feet of the left front i.e., chiefly the CPI(M). This time by passing the bill for returning the lands of the unwilling peasants Mamata Banerjee politically drove CPI(M) to the corner. CPI(M) is now realising that in case they decide to oppose the bill they will be far more isolated from the masses. This is the reason why ethically they failed to oppose this bill inside the Assembly. This is also the reason why the previous Land Minister of the region Abdur Rejjak Molla has been compelled to comment in the Assembly that 'I am congratulating the Trinamool Chief Minister for taking this initiative.' The leader of the Opposition Suryakanta Misra has also observed that from the moral point of view, we are also not opposing, the Bill. It is in this question that people have given their verdict against us. The Forward Block MLA Akshay Thakur has also confessed that it is because we turned a deaf ear to the weepings of the peasants that we are today in the opposition bench. The political success of Mamata Banerjee consists in the fact that standing on the floor of the Assembly she has succeeded in making the opposition legislators including the opposition leader to admit their political mistakes.

In her Assembly speech Mamata Banerjee informed the House that in Tamil Nadu, by way of amending the law, the peasants have been given lease of the land. But the present alliance government of the region is desirous to give the peasants not land on lease but the ownership of land. This assurance of the Chief Minister has infinite importance. By giving ownership of lands to the peasants she is actually trying to establish the rights of the peasants in the agricultural lands. At the same time she has also informed that very soon a package will also be declared for the agricultural workers in Singur. This declaration of the Chief Minister is also very momentous. Only the life and livelihood of the owners of the land do not depend on the agricultural land, but it is connected with the future of numerous agricultural workers.

As a result of the acquisition of agricultural lands in Singur not only the future of the owners of land became uncertain but also thousands of agricultural workers were faced with a crisis. While acquiring the lands, the previous left front government did not take into consideration the plight of these impoverished agricultural workers. Mamata Banerjee has to be thanked not only for the reason that she was concerned with the interest of the owners of land alone but she has also attached due importance to the circumstances of the hapless agricultural workers as well.

Of course the MLA of Singur Rabindra Nath Bhattacharya has raised an important question. He said that adequate importance should be attached separately to the cases of those unwilling peasants who were pressurised to accept the cheques of compensation. Rabindranath Babu is quite justified in making this observation. It may be reasonably expected that the new government would pay due consideration to the fact that such peasants are not deprived in any way.

This historic Bill of Singur is not only the victory of the peasants of Singur, but also it is the victory of the peasant community in all the corners of the country. It is the victory of the peasant movement.

This victory will be recorded in letters of gold in the history of the peasant movement of the nation.

15

SPOTLIGHT ON JUDICIARY

In all the regions of India including West Bengal three crores of cases have already been accumulated in all the legal institutions. These statistics were recently quoted by the Chief Minister Mamata Banerjee who observed that in cases of necessity the 'Shift System' may be introduced in the different courts of the region. At the same time she has laid stress on the need for infrastructural development in the legal institutions.

Inaugurating a meeting in the Kolkata High Court in order to implement the project for reducing the number of cases pending in the entire legal system the Chief Minister opined that the infrastructural circumstances in different courts in the region are deplorable. There is acute shortage of space. Many of the judges do not receive vehicular facilities. True, there are ample men for operating the computers, but the thing to deplore is that there is an acute scarcity in the number of computers. A few days ago the Law Minister went on a business to the Bankshall Court and he has submitted a report regarding the mismanagement prevailing there. The Chief Minister commented that very soon e-governance has to be introduced in the courts. She informed that she has already issued the necessary instruction in this regard.

In another function on the occasion of the 150th Year of the High Court, the Chief Minister commented that the regional government is desirous of drawing up a housing project for the lawyers and the members of the judiciary. The Law Minister Malay Ghatak who was also present on the occasion was given the necessary instruction to this effect.

She made the further comment that we must also keep in mind

the very vital question of the security of the lawyers. They have no post-retirement security. All the government employees enjoy the benefits of pension, P.F. and gratuity. But the lawyers have no such benefits. Something should be done for these people and the members of their families. So many years have elapsed since the attainment of independence but it is strange that even today there is acute scarcity of toilet facilities in the court premises.

It is also strange that so far nobody bothered himself over all such matters. The new government will however pay adequate attention to these problems. If we can cooperate with the Kolkata High Court, it will raise its head further and show the proper direction to the region. 'Own your Own Housing' scheme will be introduced for the benefit of the lawyers. She observed that not much land is required in such projects. It is the government who will procure the land and also assume the responsibility of building the houses. There will be three or four categories of houses. So that the persons concerned will be enabled to purchase houses according to his or her financial capabilities.

Commenting on the question of insurance and other projects, she observed that the main problem in this matter was that accurate statistics in this respect were unavailable and nobody knows for certain how many lawyers are there in the region, She advised the Law Minister Malay Ghatak to make the necessary inquiries in this matter.

Commenting on the problem of so many cases pending in the courts, she observed that if three or four judges are accommodated in a police vehicle, their efficiency and work-capacity are bound to suffer. Of course there is scarcity of financial resources but we must try our level best to solve the problems. She informed that 151 fast track courts of the region were closed down. But from the month of March necessary directions have been given to reopen them for at least 1 year.

The Central Law Minister Birappa Moili inaugurated the project for reducing the pending cases and commented that "Within six months i.e. within December 31 attempts will be made to reduce pending cases in the *lower* courts to the extent of 40%. The task is difficult but we are optismistic if everything goes well, 2/3rds of the undertrial prisoners w*ill* be released", Moili informed that the number of undertrial prisoners in the entire country is 8 lakh. For the infrastructural development of the lower courts, Rs. 21,000 crores had been granted. In case more finance was required, appeal should be made to the Central Finance Minister. He informed that it was a matter for hope that the Chief Justices of 21 High Courts of the country have taken initiatives in implementing these projects. As things stand today only 5% of the total number of persons desirous of availing themselves of the legal facilities can go to the courts. The door of judicial facilities should be opened to more and more people.

16

RATIONALE OF SECOND CHAMBER

Mamata Banerjee's Government wants to revive the Legislative Council in West Bengal which was closed down by Jatin Chakravarti in the Period of Jyoti Basu. This, however, is not a new decision. The programme to revive the Legislative Council was included in the list of electoral assurances of the Trinamool Congress. That is why the new Chief Minister will perhaps aver that she is only desirous of fulfilling her earlier promises.

But the problem involved in this connexion cannot be overlooked. This assurance was in reality the outcome of a misguided mindset. If this decision is actually translated into action West Bengal will be confronted with a disaster. If on the contrary it is judiciously given the go-bye, the region will derive ample benefits in the long run. A section of the ruling party or the critics of the party chief will explain that the sole purpose behind reviving this already defunct institution is to please the favourite persons of the chief minister. It is however not known for certain whether this impression is true or false. But the tendency to find out a motive behind all activities is actually a kind of meanness. This malady should be avoided like a poison. The objection against the revival of Legislative Council comes not from a mean attitude of mind. It is actually an ethical issue in character. In a pluralistic political setup the upper chamber is superfluous precisely because it involves unnecessary financial burdens which should punctiliously be curtailed in a poverty-ridden regional economy of a developing subcontinent.

The model of representative plurality which is prevalent in our country presupposes the existence of a legislative Assembly at the regional level and the Loksabha at the national level. These institutions are entrusted with the function of Legislature. In case there is a Second Chamber in the Legislature it reduces the status of this institution. It is due to this reason that not only the Legislative Council of a region but also the Rajya Sabha at the national level is considered as detrimental and also inessential. What is actually the purpose of these institutions and what is their rationale ? Whom do the members of these bodies really represent ? Whatever be the actual mode of their election they will have to be indirectly worked upon as people's representative. In a democracy there cannot be any other mode of moral sanction behind becoming a member of the Legislative Assembly. But the direct representatives of the people are the members of the Loksabha and Vidhansabha. And by virtue of what moral right will the indirectly elected popular representatives attenuate the gravity of the directly elected representatives.

The answer to this question is familiar. It is pleaded that the members of the Rajya Sabha or the Vidhan Parishad are comparatively speaking wiser, shrewd and senior in thoughts. They will definitely enrich the legislative process through their intellectual abilities. But this is a fallacious argument. In the first place both in the Loksabha and Vidhansabha there exist committees for different purposes which consider various legal proposals. These committees are constituted with veteran popular representatives or at least that should be the case. That is why there is no necessity for setting up an additional chamber for the purpose of monitoring and review. Secondly, there is little necessity for accomodating experts or intellectuals in different matters for knowing their opinions in the Rajya Sabha or the Vidhan Parishad. The Government or the legislature can always adorably adopt their advices. In cases of necessity specific committees can be set up with their associates. The new Government in West Bengal has already considerable experience in this respect. A possible argument in favour of the Rajya Sabha would be advanced if there was the provision of equal numbers of reprosentives for each of the component regions of the Indian federation in the pattern of the American Senate or, in other words if the importance of Uttar Pradesh and Mizoram in the Rajya Sabha were equal to each other. In that case the Rajya Sabha would really become the representative of the component regions.

In U.S.A. the Senate has its own logic. But it did not happen in the case of India. Like the Lok Sabha in the Rajya Sabha as well the number of members of the component regions has been fixed in proportion to the population. Consequently the Rajya Sabha has been reduced to a replica of the Lok Sabha. This also is not enough. Mamata Banerjee will not be able to advance this theoretical and probable argument in favour of the Vidhan Parishad if of course she does not intend to view the Vidhan Parishad as a representative of the districts. That is why she should immediately desist from her attempt to revive the Legislative Council. On the contrary she should concentrate her efforts to convert the Legislative Assembly in an arena of ideal democratic debates. Such efforts will not only initiate a process of transformation in West Bengal but will also lead the remaining nation on the path of democracy i.e. a Government by debate discussion and dialogue as opposed to an autocratie type of Government.

17

FINANCIAL SQUABBLES : DIFFICULT CHALLENGE AHEAD

So long the outgoing Finance Minister of West Bengal - Asim Dasgupta was unwilling to admit the truth that they have drained off the public exchequer. Even the other day the outgoing Chief Minister was uttering words of hollow assurance that 'everything was in right order'. The real truth however was that people like Buddhadeva Babu and Asim Babu had the wrong notion that all along they would succeed in befooling the citizens of the region by sitting on a mountain of falsehoods and hiding all the truth from public view. But an unpalatable truth is that one hardly enjoys happy days forever. A person who was at the peak of affluence yesterday may today become a discarded person in public estimation. After Buddhadeva Babu and Asim Babu have been dislodged from their pedestals of power in the Writers Building as a result of the blast of winds of change, it is understood that they have made the region totally bankrupt. It is a matter of wonder that these misdeeds of the earlier ministers have been made public by the very bureaucrats of the previous government. The Economic Report which these bureaucrats have submitted to the new government indicates that the administration left behind by Buddhadeva Bhattacharya and Asim Dasgupta etc. is literally bankrupt.

In order to review the present financial circumstances of the regional government, the Finance Secretary Chanchalmal Bachhawat recently convened a conference. The picture of financial impoverishment of the region is clear from that conference. Already a debt of 2 lakh crores of rupees has been incurred by the regional government. Over and above that an amount of about Rs. 2800 crores will have to be procured by it at the beginning of June as the salaries and pensions for the month of May. Money has got to be collected for the payment of arrears of the government creditors. The quantum of this money exceeds Rs. 5000 crores. Over and above that there are no accounts of Rs. 480 crores taken as advances from different government treasuries. On the eve of the election this acute financial crisis prompted Asim Dasgupta to stop the works of different developmental projects. Payments of the bills of the contractors employed in these projects were stopped. Consequently the activities relating to East-West Metro, Jawaharlal Nehru all-India Urban Development, Ganga Action Plan and the construction of the different roads and bridges were faced with a deep crisis.

In order to reactivate these developmental projects the new government will have first to make the payment of the bills of the contractors. Taken all things together men like Asim Babu have gifted a difficult situation to the new government.

This financial crisis of the region did not happen overnight. The unwise decision that had been followed by the regional government is responsible for this miserable plight of West Bengal. For quite a few number of years Asim Babu tried to hide this bankruptcy from public gaze by giving sheer bluff in the name of submitting a zero-deficit budget. But even in this way he failed to hide the poverty of West Bengal. Rather the more this destitution became self-evident, the more vocal had become the Finance Minister in his misconceived efforts in denying the real circumstances. Sometimes he accused the deprivation of the Centre. Sometimes he described the situation as make-believe propaganda of the Opposition. But what is true can not be concealed forever. The cat that men like Asim Babu kept hidden so far has at last come out of the bag.

Men like Asim Babu wholly neglected the question of development of this region for all these thirty four or thirty five years. No holistic programme was adopted for enhancing the income of the region. It was the official statistics which disclosed that in West Bengal debts have mounted more in comparison to the hike in annual internal productions. It is for a pretty long time that West Bengal had been suffering from a pathetic disequilibrium between public revenue and expenditure. The real truth was that in the name of giving services men like Asim Babu spent up the entire government finance in the act of maintaining the party cadres. It was as a result of expenditure in the unproductive account that the public treasury has been emptied. No positive programmes were ever adopted by them for increasing the public revenue. And this is the reason for the anemia of the regional government. This destitution is therefore all too evident at present.

Under such circumstances the new government under the leadership of Mamata Banerjee has assumed the charges of administration. After it is installed in power the first challenge before the new government will be to free the region from this economic crisis. It is impossible for even the Almighty to alter overnight the economic circumstances of the region which is gasping under the burden of a debt of Rs. 2 lakh crores. There can be no gainsaying the fact that the new government will have to undertake inhuman efforts to remove this burden and fill up once again the public exchequer. Much circumspection and much discretion will be necessary for tackling this hazardous situation. From the very beginning the new government will have to make wise endeavours for meeting the huge burden left behind by the people like Buddhadeva Babu and Asim Babu.

18

ROAD TO SOLUTION

On 7th June, 2011 within three weeks of sitting in the chair of the chief minister in Writers Building Mamata Banerjee entered into a treaty with the leaders of Janamukti Morcha and declared that the problems of the Hills have been solved. This was certainly an exaggeration. Because a treaty and a solution are hardly synonymous, a treaty is in fact only a step, towards a solution. If the bipartite treaty of the month of June was the first step the tripartite treaty of July 18,2011 which took place between the national government, the regional government and the Morcha is of course the second step. The Gorkhaland Territorial Administration (GTA) may not be the last answer to the problems of the Hills but if we advance in quest of a solution in this path its importance in the history of solution of a long undecided problem is undeniable.

Apparently the conflict between the regional government and Janamukti Morcha during the period of the leftist government reached an 'insoluble' stage. It appeared that the distance between the two sides can never be bridged up. In order to overcome such distance in political affairs each side has to concede some grounds to the demands of the other. It can also be described as an act of compromise but in a positive sense. The GTA treaty of course consists of such a compromise. The regional government has acceded to the demands of Morcha to a considerable extent, allowed the right of autonomy or self-administration and even raised no objection to the inclusion of the word 'Gorkhaland'. The Morcha also remained inhibited from the repitition of the demand for a seperate region. This is indeed a good augury.

But there is of course some apprehension between the treaty

and the consequence. For the time being Bimal Gurung is positive, considerate and in the middle position. So far so good. But it is difficult to ascertain whether he will remain stable in this position. Because the politics which he practises is usually adverse to the middle position and has a normal tendency to move towards an extreme position.

The rise of Bimal Gurung in the place of Subash Ghishing has partially proved this proposition. If in the future the Morcha leaves the middle path and once again raises the demand for a separate region the whole process of establishment of peace will be at stake. And its impact will be felt in the Plains. The Plains are already full of unrest, simmering with discontent and in this fire fuel is being provided by party politics. Such a situation will continue for long.

In the first phase Mamata Banerjee has shown discretion to tackle this conflict, particularly in the signature ceremony of this Tripartite Treaty she has sat by the side of Bimal Gurung and Roshan Giri to emphasise the existence of undivided West Bengal and the good relation between the Hills and the Plains. We can only expect that this wisdom will be victorious in the long run.

But wisdom alone, though necessary, is not sufficient. It must be accompanied by development. In the tripartite treaty the outline of development is well defined and substantial. Not only is there a programme of allotment of finance, the liberty to utlise that finance has also been proposed. If this liberty is utilised properly, if unlike in their past the greater part of this allotted finance is not strayed through corrupt practices, if the rate of socio-economic development of the people of the Hills is actually accelerated, then that will be the real long term strategy of the development of the Hills. If the leaders of the Hills and the Plains irrespective of their factional differences can forget their small and short-run differences and become partners of that develoment Darjeeing need not be converted into Switzerland; it can automatically become a symbol of peace and stability and it is only then that the problems of the Hills will be solved in the truest sense.

19

RESOLUTIONS OF NEW MINISTRY

On May 19, 20th the new Ministry under the leadership of Mamata Banerjee took oath in the Rajbhavan and immediately thereafter in the first conference of the Ministry the following resolutions were adopted. For example, (1) the contents of the agreement with the Tatas over the lands at Singur will be made public, (2) the report of the Sachar committee for the development of the Muslim Community will be implemented, (3) the direction for recovering all kinds of illegal armaments will be declared, (4) impartiality in administration will be brought back instead of blind allegiance to the party, (5) accurate identity cards will be arranged for the persons living below the poverty line and the deficiencies will be corrected in the matter of allocating hundred days' work, (6) review committee will be constituted for releasing the political prisoners, (7) collective efforts will be undertaken with the Home Ministry in the matter of disaster management, (8) a separate secretariat will be constituted for the development of North Bengal (9) attempts will be made to solve the problems of the Hills as well as Jangalmahal within three months, (10) the press corner before the chamber of the Chief Minister in the Writers Building which was broken down in the leftist regime will be reconstructed. There is little doubt that most of these decisions are related with the interests of the impoverished working people of West Bengal. The point to note at present is whether the new government is really sincere about their implementation.

It is of course true that there are many difficult challenges before the new regional government. In the first place it is not easy to reactivate the administrative machinery, which was converted into a static and blind lackey of the ruling party during the last thirty three or thirty four years. For about three and a half decades in this region all the governmental activities were conducted effectively by the direction of CPI (M). It was the leaders of CPI (M) who treated the district magistrates, subdivisional officers and the administrators and police officials of all levels as the lackeys of their own party. In every activity the permission of the party activists rather than the recommendations of the government has served as the green signal. The matter has assumed an uglier shape at the civic and panchayat levels. Lakhs of rupees from the public treasury have been squandered there in a planned manner. Decade after decade this menace has vitiated the administration in West Bengal and also caused a rot in the entire social system, starting from health and education in all the departments relating to public interest there has taken place the interference of the party activists. It is really difficult to move forward by breaking this deadlock or vicious circle.

For a long time the people of this region yearned for a really unrestricted and transparent election. This demand became far stronger than earlier after the panchayat, Loksabha and the civic elections. In this year's Assembly polls Qureshi's Election Commission tried to fulfil this demand of the citizens of West Bengal to the best of its ability. After many years the ordinary voters in the district areas are happy to cast their own votes. Many year later there has occurred a mass uprising in the voting machine. And in that connection a new government has come into power - a government which is truly elected by the verdict of the majority of the voters.

But it should not be forgotten that who had been continuously in power in the region since 1977 were not wholly lonely. Impelled by the urge to hold power in their hands for year after year, they created numerous pressure groups at different levels of the social and governmental system. They have themselves relished the taste of power and nourished these pressure groups with fertilizers and water. It is true that in comparison with the lakhs of crores of people of the region the people of these quarters are less numerous. But by virtue of their movement for long at different levels of the governmental and administrative structures they are quite familiar with the nuances of the governmental activities. When they will find that the impartial activities of the new government are proving to be a stumbing block to their long-drawn-out habits of serving their own interests, they will make utmost efforts to hinder all these activities. The new ministry will have to take into account all these possible hazards in a cool brain.

Ordinary citizens are aware that the CPI(M) government of the last regime has drained off the life-bloods of the region. They are aware of the burden of 2 lakh crores of rupees of the region. The vehicle in which the new ministry has ascended is totally ramshackle. Even the optimism of the crores of the citizens of the region is not sufficient to provide motion to this car. But people will be happy if it observes that the new government is at least repairing its obsolescent machinery and making efforts to put new life into it. Its sincere efforts will convince the citizens that the new government is at least not lacking in political good will. Unlike the previous government the new authorities are not intent upon making scapegoats of the ordinary citizens.

20

NOT JUST BLIND ALLEGIANCE

On the very second day of taking oath as the Chief Minister Mamata Banerjee has declared that not blind allegiance to the party but competence will be taken by her administration as the criterion of efficiency. She will admire the efficiency and dexterity of the public workers as well as the officers and will not go into the analysis of the question of a person's political allegiance. At the same time the new Chief Minister has issued a directive to the government officers, she has said that within seven days the government officers will have to inform which department is in which stage. Within seven days a blueprint of action should be drawn up. There is no doubt that this declaration on the very second day of being installed into power will create hopes among the citizens at large. Everybody will extend thanks to the sincerity of the new government. If the image of the unbiased and transparent administration which disappeared from the region can be made to return by the new Chief Minister her slogan of bringing about a 'change' will be fruitful in all manners. The people who entrusted Mamata Banerjee with the changes of the Chief Minister and installed her in the Writers Building are desirous to see that 'change' should come not only in the colour of the government but also in its modus operand. This declaration of Mamata Banerjee has given due honour to that demand of the populace.

During the last thirty four years the citizens of this region were totally oblivious of the transparent and dynamic image of the administration which is above the cult of party allegiance. During the leftist regime of this long period the government used to be controlled by Alimuddin street. No trace of an impartial government could be observed anywhere. The promotion of the officers took place not on the basis of efficiency or competence but the extent of intimacy of an official with Alimuddin street. Consequently the government officers gained the impression that salvation is possible only by lubricating the authorities of the Alimuddin street. And that is why accountability to Alimuddin instead of the people at large came to assume prime importance. Not only the officrs of the Writers Building but also the question of putting the officers in important positions was determined by Alimuddin street. It was Alimuddin Street which decided who will become the vice-chancellor of which university. The direction of Alimuddin Street was indispensable for deciding which particular person will be selected for becoming the chairman of a committee or a commission. In this way blind party allegiance came to permeate the administration from top to bottom. Naturally the question of efficiency and competence was pushed to the background. For the simple reason of being intimate to the party unworthy mediocre people became important at all the levels of the administration. Its inevitable impact in the administration was also conspicuous.

The citizens of the region observed an one-eyed incapable administration. In reality CPI(M) never gifted a people's government to the inhabitants of the region, What CPI(M) gave the region was a biased CPI(M) government.

It is this scandalous situation in the administion which Mamata Banerjee has taken the initiative to remedy. Mamata is well aware that the tasks which were left untouched by the perfunctory performance of the Left Front government will have to be completed by her. It is with that expectation that the people of West Bengal have sent her to the Writers' Building. In order to fulfil that expectation she needs first of all a dynamic transparent and capable administration which will work in the interest of the people. With that end in view the government officers should be accorded responsibility in terms of efficiency and competence. So long as this is not performed the government cannot be made dynamic and workworthy. This is the reason why the new Chief Minister has laid emphasis on the question of administrative reform by giving recognition to the factors of efficiency and dexterity.

The predecessor of Mamata Banerjee, Buddhadeva Bhattacharya raised the slogan 'Do it now'. But his slogan was reduced to a farce. He failed to transform even an iota of the work culture of the government officers. The misbehaviour that was meted out to ordinary people in government offices was continued in the period of Buddhadeva Bhattacharya. The dillydallying modus operandi of the government offices of the previous period were repeated in the period of Buddhadeva Babu. The truth is that Buddhadeva Babu failed to release his government from the clutches of the party. That is why he did not have the courage to give due recognition to questions of efficiency and competence. In fact he had to give leadership to an unworthy and inept government.' On the contrary Mamata Banerjee did not raise any catchy slogan. But she has made it clear that she will take stern steps in gifting the people a dynamic and workworthy government. This firm and liberal outlook is her hallmark. If she really succeeds in breaking the deadlock of 34 years and brings in West Bengal the flood of a new work culture the people of this region will remain grateful to her for all times to come.

21

TIMELY WARNING

On July 21, 2011 in the vast mass meeting of the party in the Brigade Parade Ground the Trinamool Congress supremo Mamata Banerjee has unleashed a warning against her opponent CPI (M) and also alerted the activists and supporters of her own party. In this meeting of July 21 the TMC supremo has announced that instances of corruption and bossing in her party will never be tolerated. Any kinds of factional politics in her party will also not be tolerated. All such instances will be suitably punished.

Mamata Banerjee has also made it clear that she dislikes the ideal that the leaders of the party will unnecessarily poke their noses in the business of the government. She has reminded everybody that no one should rake up any disorder in the hospitals or health centres. In case there is uncleanliness the party activists should themselves put their hands in cleaning them up. The TMC supremo has also warned the party activists not to get embroiled in the politics of retribution. She has said that no one should create disorder or kill the CPI (M) activists. They have already been adequately punished by the citiezens of the region in the electoral warfare. Instead of running after money TMC activists should learn to stand by the side of the ordinary citizens. In her own characteristic style in the Brigade Parade Ground she has made her party people take oath that unlike CPI (M) Trinamool Congress will never steal nor commit murder. The very words which were expected from her as a responsible leader were uttered by Mamata Banerjee in the Brigade Parade Ground. These words will give solace to the citizens of the region. In fact Mamata Banerjee is aware that after assuming administrative power of the region her responsibility has much enhanced.

She has realised that the citizens of the region did not only yearn for a change in the outward form of the government. A change was sought in the political culture which struck root in this region for the last decades. It is this yearning which has impelled the citizens of this region to give unstinted support to her party and her party in this year's Assembly election. Mamata Banerjee knows how to honour this demand of the populace.

The deficiencies about which Mamata Banerjee alerted her party activists in the Brigade Parade Ground meeting were responsible for this sorry plight of CPI(M). She has warned the Trinamool Congress not to run after money. In the last three decades CPI(M) went away from the side of the people and was converted into a party whose chief objective became earning money by hook or by crook. This observation applies to all sorts of CPI(M) leaders, big, small or middle. Conse quently they are submerged in corruption and gave encouragement to corruption at all levels. Mamata Banerjee has warned that bossing by the party activists will not be tolerated any more. Every where beginning from the local clubs or school committees to government offices or educational institutions the CPI(M) leaders have exercised their authority. And in cases of lack of allegiance to the CPI(M) leaders hard punishments were awarded.

The citizens of the region failed to tolerate this unbridled corruption and authoritarian attitude of the CPI(M) leaders and that is why with the revival of 'free and fair'voting system they have thrown away the yoke of this corrupt regime. With the expectation and of the conclusion of corruption and authoritarianism that men have given unstinted support to Trinamool Congress.

People have witnessed the failure of the CP(M) leadership to stop the prevalence of corruption and authoritarianism.They correctly understood that outwardly CP(M) speaks of purification campaigns but in actual fact gives indulgence to instances of corruption and authoritarianism. That is why the electorate refused to be led along the gardenpath in this year's election. Rather they turned a deaf ear to the slogan of 'purification'and have given abundant support Mamata Banerjee understands well that at the end of the leftist regime of three decades her first and foremost duty is to present a transparent and uncorrupt administration and to stop the authoritarian activities of the ruling party in different areas.

At the Brigade Parade Ground meeting she has given indication of this determination. Mamata is also aware that in Trinamol Congress she happens to be the first person and she also happens to be the last. The rest are only her shadows. She alone is responsible for all the successes ofTrinamool Congress. Similarly, if there is the slightest disorder in this party people will point an accusing finger at Mamata Banerjee. That is why she will have to remain alert always and hold the reins of the party with capable hands, If she really succeeds in this difficult task she will be marked as an exceptional ruler in regional politics and she will never have to look back.

22

A TRULY WISE STEP: NOT JUST ANOTHER GIMMICK

During the last few days after assuming the charge of the chief minister of West Bengal Mamata Banerjee has taken a few most important administrative decisions. Among these decisions are : arranging payment of monthly salary to the teachers and the non-teaching staff on the first day of the month, payment of salary and allowances to the government servants through the banks, increase of budget allowances to the North Bengal Development Board, allotment of Rs. 40 crores as food subsidies to backward areas and BPL consumers, taking the advices of the experts for saving the region from incidence of flood and drought etc. All these administrative decissions adopted by the new chief minister are undoubtedly highly populist. Over and above that, all these decisions are fruits of deep and far-reaching reflection. All these decisions are giving the impression that Mamata Banerjee instead of being concerned with instantaneous profits is far more eager to derive future benefits.

Another such constructive decision has also been recently announced by Mamata Banerjee. She has announced that without the collective decision of the regional ministry the Municipality or the Municipality Department is not entitled to allot any land. In other words, Mamata has brought the right to allot lands into the hands of the ministry.The Municipal and Urban Development Minister Firhad Hakim has informed the people of this decision of the chief minister and said that nobody could allot the lands the Municipalities of the region including Salt Lake according to their own free will. Before allotting the lands the matter should be recommended by the regional cabinet. Neither the Municipality Department nor the Municipalities will any longer have the right to distribute lands in their own hands.

There are two possible consequences of this decision. Firstly, as a result of this decision it would be possible to resist unplanned urban development. It would also be possible to know where and how much land is there in the hands of the government. Secondly, speculative activities and corrupt practices around lands can be resisted to a great extent.

There can be no gainsaying the fact that so far as a result of retaining unrestricted rights of land distribution in the hands of the Municipalities and the Municipality Department hindrances were created in the road to planned urban development. In many cases different municipalities allocated lands according to their sweet will. In many cases in times of necessity private lands were not available. What is more, no clear account of where and how much land was in the hands of the government was available. As a result of the new decision it would be possible for the government to understand where and how much land is in its hand. The government would also realise how that land can be utilised according to plan. By utilising these lands properly in a planned manner the government can instil discipline into urban development.

Along with planned urban development as a result of this governmental decision speculative activities and corrupt practices around land would also be resisted to a greatest extent. During the leftist regime a dishonest circle of speculators around land grew up throughout the region. Many bigwigs of the ruling party also were involved in that circle. The left front minister took the decision that unutilised government khasland should be distributed among the shelterless at Re. 1 only. Apparently this decision of the last government seemed to be a populist move. Actually, however, this was a secret ploy to manipulate the vote bank. More than that, as a result of that decision of the government the circle of people who found indulgence of the party in land speculation in different areas, instead of the poor people derived extra benefits.

On the one hand, these people deprived the really indigent persons and obtained vast tracts of land under false names. On the other hand they have deprived the real patta-recievers and kept the government documents in their own possessions and earnt lakhs of rupees by selling that same lands to others at high prices. Since during the last regime there were no regulations in the allocation of lands these speculators and their dapendent mastans (ruffians) uttered the last words. Murders and incidents of violence around lands were rife. And throughout the region almost everywhere above their heads there was the umbrella of the ruling party CP (M).

Apparently, the present decision of the new government may not appear to be a populist decision. But a little reflection will convince anybody that a constructive outlook is working behind this decision. Constructive activity means very often avoidance of the path of cheap popularity. The present government of course deserves our thanks for deviating from the cheap and popular path of land allocation of the left front government. The circle of dishonest speculators which has grown up around land distributors throughout the length and breadth of the region should be broken up for ensuring proper utilisation of land and this will open up the path of genuine development.

23

VISIT TO HOSPITAL

On Saturday, July 2, 2011, Mamata Banerjee paid a surprise visit to the B.C. Roy Children's Hospital and this has solved many longstanding problems. Following her advice in order to resist the sudden "referring" of the sick children, the system of 'teleconferencing' of the B.C. Roy Hospital to the hospitals at the district, sub division and block levels is being introduced. At a particular time of the day, the teachers and the physicians of the Roy Children's Hospital will talk through this teleconferencing system with the pediatricians of these hospitals and give them necessary advice.

Apart from that in order to restore the work culture in the hospital, necessary directions have been issued this day for timely attendance of the physicians and health workers. It has been declared that in case of misbehaviour with the guardians of the children, the physicians and nurses may be given hard punishment.

The scarcity of ambulance in this largest hospital for children's treatment is a longstanding problem. There was no police stations in the vicinity in order to resist any problem of law and order. After the surprise visit of the Chief Minister, two ambulances have been allotted for the hospital as per the direction of the Chief Minister. New officers have been appointed for the police outpost on this very day.

Apart from that responding to the appeal of the hospital authorities, the Chief Minister also gave the green signal for purchasing machinery worth Rs. 1 crore 36 lakhs for the sick new born care unit under construction. Among these instruments are USG machine, pulse oximeter infusion pump, monitor etc. The parents of children were panic-stricken for the death of 19 children in two days. They all heaved a sigh of relief at the arrival of the Chief Minister.

The Principal, Dr. Mrinalkanti Chatterjee observed that as a result of sudden visit of the C.M. there would be much advantages in adopting adequate measures against the derelict physicians and the health workers. He added that in order that the new mothers could learn to cook nutritious food at less cost, we were starting a nutritious rehabilitation centre at Beliaghata B.C. Roy Polio Hospital for the purpose of giving training.

On this day the Chief Minister remained in the B.C. Roy Hospital for 20-25 minutes. She asked the physicians many questions relating to the outdoor, emergency step down ward, different wards in the first floor, the newly born babies in the second floor and the measures adopted to save the seriously sick new born children. She inspected the neonatal and pediatric intensive care unit.

She was extremely amazed to learn that the weights of 30 newly born babies were 700-800 gms only. She observed that the weights of these children were half of those of the normal children. She commented that the real reason was that their mothers also lacked adequate nutrition. She advised the officers to adopt necessary steps for this matter.

Receiving complaints from the parents, she expressed her grievance to the journalists that there were no free beds in the hospital. In case BPL certificates could not be available within 3 days, daily bed fees had to be given to the extent of Rs. 30/. Many children have to stay in the hospital for 20 or 30 days. It is difficult for the indigent parents to procure so much money.

The Chief Minister said that there was much pressure in the hospital. Two or three children have to be kept in a bed. Most of the children were in serious condition and brought from far away areas. In certain areas of the hospital there are shortages of infrastructural facilities. Such facilities have to be expanded further. She was amazed to learn that every year 40,000 newly born babies die in this region despite the best efforts of the physicians to save them. She commented that no politicking should be made over this matter and our best wishes should be reserved in favour of these children.

24

IRON DUST SCANDAL

Another scandal which was suppressed during the leftist regime is now coming to the limelight. The chief Minister Mamata Banerjee has ordered a CID inquiry into the iron dust scandal of more than 350 crores of rupees. As per the directive of the Chief Minister, the Food Minister Jyotipriya Mallik has already prepared the necessary papers relating to that scandal. It was known that during the Beijing Olympic in 2008 India received the huge order of supplying iron dust for construction purposes. West Bengal was entrusted with the duty of supplying iron dust worth Rs. 358 crores.

In the name of supplying iron dust the Essential Commodities Supply Corporation paid this amount of money to 24 private organisations. Subsequently after consulting the necessary papers, it was discovered that not a single kilogram of iron dust was sent to China. But various organizations received payments. The managers of the organizations among whom this huge amount of money was distributed all rub shoulders with the leaders of CPM or Forward Block.

The story does not end here. The Home Department of the previous government did not give the necessary permission to the Essential Commodities Supply Corporation to submit the chargesheet against an IAS officer involved in this scandal of Rs. 350 crores. It was learnt from the Home Department itself that much hindrances used to put up in order to suppress the whole matter and protect the big shots of the previous left government from the tentacles of law.

However, this iron dust scandal is a minute fragment of the scandal relating to thousands of crores of rupees in the period of the left front. Many other such scandals are perpetrated by the previous leftist rule. And all these scandals have been suppressed in this manner. The way the previous leftist rulers sought to suppress this scandal of 350 crores of rupees indicates that in case of an inquiry many big shots will be implicated. Many dishonest activities of many people will be revealed. At the same time it will also be revealed that all these mischiefs were done in the knowledge of the government and by the encouragement of the government.

It should be remembered that the organisations which were paid Rs. 350 crores, but supplied not a single grain of iron dust simply as a result of their intimacy with the earlier ruling coterie were actually paid the money of the people. During the last three and a half years, the previous leftist government has in this way squandered vast amounts of public money. This incident is the proof that the previous leftist government in West Bengal was not innocent in comparison to the corrupt performances of the Lalu Prasad government in Bihar or the Mayabati government in Uttar Pradesh.

It is welcome that the new government in West Bengal has taken initiatives to inquire into the scandal relating to this vast amount of money. No one can give moral support to this sort of squandering of public money. It is in public interest that an inquiry must immediately be made into this scandal. At the same time hard punishments should be awarded to those who will be found guilty in the inquiry. The government will have to keep strict vigil so that any guilty bigwig cannot escape the clutches of the legal machinery.

At the same time it should be remembered that the duties of the new government will not be finished by making an inquiry into this single scandal. All the cases of corruption perpetrated during the leftist regime have to be inquired into one by one. Because it is the expectation of the people that the new government will make due inquiry into all the misdeeds of the earlier government, identify the guilty people and give them adequate punishment. The new government must of necessity remedy the injustices. It may be logically expected that in case the new government makes inquiry into all the scandals of the previous leftist regime, many bigwigs will be implicated and many secret stories of squandering the public money will come to the limelight.

25

HEALTH SERVICES IN THE BALANCE

On 31st May, 2011 the Chief Minister Mamata Banerjee announced a few measures for the development of the health infrastructure of the region. She has informed that in Jangalmahal four super speciality hospitals will be set up, a programme for setting up a modern hospital at Rajarhat has been adopted for neurological treatment, at Bhowanipore a 300-bed orthopaedic hospital will be set up, the programme for setting up a separate hospital for women is considered and along with these all the district hospitals and primary health centres will be modernised.

The chief minister has kept the charge of the Health Department in her own hands. In the mean time she has made an on-the-spot inspection of four hospitals of Kolkata. She is trying to find out exactly where the shoe pinches in the Health Department. It may be presumed that after assuring the responsibility of the new government she is certainly realising that the health infrastructure of the region is totally deficient. Bringing back this deficient health system to the proper position on a wartime footing should occupy the foremost position in the list of priorities of the regional government.

The imbalance in the health circumtances of the region has been discussed many times earlier. No body has expressed satisfaction on that score. As in other spheres of social services the earlier leftist rulers have irrationally injected party politics into the health services too for the last three and a half decades and thus inflicted infinite damage on the entire system.

In other regions the governments always give a high prority to the sphere of health and medicine. But in the left front regime in West Bengal no Health Minister was found to concern himself with the health services. Consequently there has been continuous deterioration in the government hospitals and health centres. The business of private hospitals and nursing homes has flourished. Gradually the health services have gone out of the reach of the economically weaker section and the lower middle classes of the people. People have lost confidence in the system of health and medicine of this region and started depending upon the southern regions. The new chief minister has raised the question why the helpless people of this region should go to Vellore for medical treatment? This question is quite justified. Not that such questions were never raised during the last 34 years, but the left front government paid no heed to it. The authorities of the left front government never perceived that if the citizens of this region, in want of adequate health services, set out for a different region it is an object of shame for the regional government. In fact the feelings of the authorities of the left front were totally distorted.

It is really a good indication that the new chief minister-cum-health minister has taken initiatives to alter the health circumstances. If she suceeds in this task the inhabitants of this region will derive ample benefits. They will no longer have to start for other regions for good treatment. If the conditions prevailing in the government hospitals and health centres really improve, the indigent and lower middle classes of people will no longer feel helpless in case of illness.

But at the same time the new chief minister will also have to remember that the mere introduction of a few new hospitals will not be able to improve the standard of health services in the region. In order to perform this task successfully the state of work culture of all those persons who are connected with the health services must be altered. The spirit of public service must be aroused in their minds. It is the misfortune of this region that involvement in political activities in hospitals and health centres was responsible for the vanishing of this spirit from the minds of the health activists.

Under the indulgence of the party bosses of CP(M) the hospitals and health centres were converted into the centres of reckless hullabaloo of a kind of health activists and of various corrupt practices. Whenever the ordinary citizens visit the government hospitals for availing medical treatment they used to be degraded, humiliated and defrauded at the hands of the former.

In order to alter these circumstances the chief minister will have first of all to remedy this situation. Undoubtedly this is a very serious task. It is also certain that this will compel the chief minister to face different kinds of hazards. Still this-task has of course to be performed. Otherwise truly efficient health services will remain for ever a distant dream to the citizens of this region. At the same time another task which the government should perform is to improve the standards of performance of primary health centres and district hospitals so that the pressures on the government hospitals of the Kolkata city may be reduced.

No one can deny that the health circumstances prevailing in this region cannot be improved overnight. This is indeed a matter of longrun programming. If such planning is kept at the top of the list of priorities and the long term planning is successfully implemented, the sorry plight of the inhabitants of this region can be mitigated to a considerable extent.

26

MORE ON HEALTH SERVICES

Every step of the Chief Minister Mamata Banerjee indicates that she is much concerned about the health services of the region and she is constant by thinking about how this disorderly health system can be put to order at the earliest convenience. Chief Minister Mamata Banerjee has kept the Health Department in her own hands. During the last 34 years in the left front regime the health services of the region were in total shambles - the new chief minister knows that it is not possible to repair the system overnight. And she is also aware that however impossible she will have to make it possible. It may not be done in one day but gradually the circumstances have to be improved. Active steps for this purpose should start being taken from right now. The new chief minister is well aware that among the foremost demands of the citizens of West Bengal is to bring about improvement in the deficient health services and provide really satisfactory medical treatment to the umpteen millions of the citizens of West Bengal.

Because of this awareness right after assuming the resposiblity of Chief Ministership Mamata Banerjee has girded up her loins to improve the state of the health services. Already she has paid sudden visits to quite a few government hospitals. With her own eyes she has observed the condition of those hospitals and listened to the allegations of the ordinary citizens. It is learnt now that after these visits of the chief minister the state of those hospitals have improved atleast to some extent. But this is hardly sufficient. In order to improve the circumstances of the health services many other things remain to be done. Along with brining about improvement in infrastructures of the hospitals change has got to be brought about in the mindsets of the physicians. They are engaged in great services in public interest has to be generated in their minds. Their devotion to duty was to be aroused and they should be pursuaded to become more human.

After visiting a few government hospitals, on June 7, 2011, Mamata Banerjee suddenly appeared in Swasthyabhaban. There she inspected all the activities in a detailed manner and entered into meetings with the officers. In such conference in Swasthyabhaban Mamata Banerjee told an important thing. She said that in government hospitals, out of temptation for commissions a few physicians ask the patients to go to outside laboratories for examining their blood and disease. What impertinance! This 40% commission system should be stopped. The chief minister's allegation about this sort of dishonest practices of certain physicians cannot be dismissed as insubstantial. Rather there is considerable truth in such allegation Many of the common men who usually come to government hospitals have the bitter experience of becoming victims of similar inhuman behaviour at the hands of certain physicians. Such people have resorted to the ignoble practice of the cut money and commission system which has inducted corrupt practices in the entire body politic. These physicians usually forget the Hippocratic oath which they have to take on the eve of entering their profession and become more concerned with looking after their business interest by exploiting the indigent and the low-income group of people. Through collusion with private nursing homes and laboratories they compel the patients to spend more for medical treatment. Consequently, it goes without saying the pockets of these physicians are inflated with the money earnt from commissions.

If we are at all determined to bring about an improvement of the health services the Administration must adopt strict measures against these dishonest physicians. The government must ensure that whenever the low-income-group and indigent people visit government hospitals for medical treatment they are not victimised by the circle of brokers or agents and their diagnosis and treatment are done inside the hospital itself. If any case of detection of a physician of a government hospital of enjoying 'commission' comes to the notice of the appropriate authorities punitive measures against him should be adopted instantaneously.

It was for a long time that this system of 'Commission Raj' was being practised by a class of doctors and health activists in the government hospitals. The earlier left front government used to connive at them. Because so long they had continued to conduct their illegal business through unwritten licences by showing political allegiance to the left front. The new government will have to remedy this menace in the government hospitals. The words uttered by the chief minister in the Swasthya Bhaban contains a kind of warning as well as a kind of threatening. This warning as well as threatening was really necessary for the dishonest circle of the medical people. If this warning as well as threatening does not bear fruit the chief minister must adopt far more stringent measures against them. Then only she will receive the heartiest thanks of the rank and file.

27

RIGHT MESSAGE FOR INDUSTRY

On July 30, 2011 the Industries Minister of the region Partha Chatterjeee has issued a clear message to the industrialists. It is that if land is taken for the purpose of industry it cannot be kept unutilised. Immediately industries have got to build up If land is taken for industry and yet industry is not built up I within the scheduled period the government will take back the land. The Industries Minister has also made it clear that housing complexes cannot be built up in the land taken for industrialisation.

After taking oath as the Chief Minister Mamata Banerjee also said the same words which were later uttered by Partha Chatterjee in his capacity as the Industries Minister. Already Mamata Banejee clearly said that after taking land for industry it should neither be kept unutilised nor utilised for residential purposes, her government will never tolerate this sort of speculative activities.

On July 30, 2011 the Industries Minister visited three industrial estates of the Howrah district and realised that it was the practice of many industrialists to take land for industrial purposes but keep it unutilised for many years. It was for this speculative attitude of these people that new lands are difficult to find for industries. After scrutinising the matter by making an on-the-spot study the Industries Minister has been annoyed and issued this clear message to the industrialists. This message of the Industries Minister is quite correct as well as timely. This message was really necessary for those industrialists who were keeping lands unutilised in this manner for speculative purposes.

During the last left front government much speculation and dishonest trades around lands have taken place. Beginning from giving pattas to indigent people and land acquisition for industrial purposes- everything was done by way of unbridled speculative activities by a kind of dishonest industrialists and land brokers in co-operation with a few leaders and ministers of CP(M). Knowing everything during the the last three decades the leaders of the left front government kept its eyes and ears closed. Mistaking this silence as indirect support these dishonest circles have continued their operations without any resistance. Administrative support has come in this manner. In order to give various advantages to this dishonest circle a quarter of the administration has rendered different illegal cooperations. After becoming the chief minister Mamata Bankerjee has paid attention to the large scandal relating to lands in this region. An inquiry into the land scandals will definitely throw light on many bigwigs. During the regime of the left front government a section of traders and industrialists have misutilised the government and misappropriated lands one after another. The earlier government had the pratice of indiscriminately distributing lands to them in the name of industry. In exchange these traders and industrialists who were close to the ruling coterie rendered different kinds of assistance to the ruling party. In reality it was seen that although land was taken in *the* name of industry nothing actually was done in this respect. Rather keeping that land unutilised they have tried to engage themselves into speculative activities. Many of them have tried to derive large profits by building up residential complexes by taking lands in the name of industry. Not only that, many of them have misappropriated the lands of closed factories for the purpose of promoting business. And in all theses matters they have received government help. We must welcome the initiative of the Industries Minister to stop this speculation around lands. At the same time the new Industries Minister must pay attention to another matter. No attempts to build up residential complexes in the lands of closed factories should be tolerated. Other rather new industries should be built up in those lands. The government should draw up a list of those industries who have taken land during the previous government in this manner but kept them unutilised. At the same time if they are unable to build industries adequate measures should be adopted to take away those lands immediately from them.

If the government can immediately resist this speculation around land two benefits will be received. In the first place, the government will no longer have to rack its brains to find out lands for industry. Secondly, if this speculation in land is really stopped in the interest of building industry employment oppornities in the region will expand very much. It is expected that Mamata Baneriee's government is proceeding in that very direction.

28

REFLECTIONS ON POLICE FORCES

During the leftist regime in his capacity as the chief minister of West Bengal Buddhadev Bhattacharya demanded that so far as the question of law and discipline was concerned his region was a veritable 'oasis' among the entire nation. The proof of this proposition was, however, bitter to the citizens of this region. For a pretty long time West Bengal remained in the front rank of those regions where the decline of law and order took place to the maximum extent. For this was resposible the administrative inefficiency as well as the shamelessly obeisant mentality and the activities of a portion of the police forces who virtually lost their honour and respects and became converted into sycophants of the ruling party. They acted like lackeys of the ruling party and following the directives of their leaders used to file false cases agaist the activists and the supporters of the opponent party, harassed them without reason, kept their eyes closed to the torments of the CP(M) activists and whenever the ordinary citizens went to the police stations to lodge complaints they were humiliated and driven out. For years in succession this was the experience of the rural masses. If in any rare case, a police officer did show the mettle to stand agaist the officious behaviour of the ruling party he was either transferred elsewhere or his life was in peril.

Day after day, night after night people have forborne much tortures and atrocities and have at last turned back and this fact has been reflected in this year's Assembly election. Lakhs of people have pressed the buttons of the voting machines and expressed their refusal to tolerate these circumstances any longer and their yearnings for an immediate change. Now the change has arrived at last. Throughout the sprawling West Bengal one after another red bastions have broken down like houses of cards. In the face of this change in the political scenario the apprehension was frequently expressed that such a change will inevitably be followed by retribution and there will be a blood-bath all around. Law and order circumstances will further deteriorate. It cannot be said that these apprehensions were totally unfounded. That is why after the election results were published many bigwigs of CP(M) in different areas went undergound for fear of retributive activities on the part of the common masses. Actually, however such things did not happen. The slogan of Trinamool 'We want change, not retribution' certainly touched the minds of the ordinary masses. The result was that the conflagration that was apprehended turned out to be false, only a few sparks were splattered here and there.

But that hardly means that within these few days the region has been converted into a Ramrajya. Starting from political murders incidents like murders of promoters, manhandling, application of force, damaging houses, dacoity etc., are happening ceaselessly. There is no indication of a decline in the incidence of the type of criminal offences. In the different district areas just as Trinamool activists are being murdered and facing assaults by the desperate CP(M) activists, CP(M) are also not being spared.

It is true that the way the incidents of CP(M) activists being attacked are publicised in the party organ gives many the impression that the region has become overnight a 'jungle-raj! 'The communists are unparalleled in exaggerated publicities of such matters. Nonetheless it is true that such matters are happening. It is not a fact that in all cases people of one party are killing the people of the other party. Behind many such cases there may be incidents of old time enmity over which political colour has been applied. The continuous experience of staying in power for thirty four years at a stretch has led to the cultivation of mutual recrimination, acrimony and enmity among the cadres of CP(M) themselves. The outbreak of such rancour and ill feelings is happening in many cases. Even in many cases of recovery of weapons, police is being informed not by outside people but by the insiders of CP(M). Taking all things together disorder and unrest are continuing to reign supreme in the district areas. This is more so in the rural areas than in the urban areas.

Therefore in tackling the law and discipline circumstances the new government will have to adopt really firm steps. Owing to the obeisant mentality of a long period the rusting of the police administration cannot be removed in the short period. But the citizens of the region will be primarily happy if they see that police is no longer judging the political colours of the offenders and promptly dealing with the complaints received.

29

REFLECTIONS ON POLICE FORCES-2

It is urgently necessary to alter the image of the police forces in West Bengal. This is the opinion of Kolkata's civil society. This opinion has been expressed on June 18, 2011 at the meeting of the civic committee which has been constituted at the initiative of Mamata Bannerjee by the police, popular representatives and distinguished citizens. Everybody has opined in that meeting that the image which police has projected before the people is not acceptable. Rather the very word 'police' generates in people's mind a peculiar feeling of panic and aversion. The participants did not forget to attract niotice to the fact that the activities of a certain section of the police is responsible for the building up of this unsavoury image.

It is in this conference that the distinguished artist Samir Aich has commented that the word 'police' is frightening to everybody. The actor and legislator Chiranjit has observed that by way of acting in the role of a police activist in the Bengali movies he has become converted into a villain in the public's eyes. It is in the presence of the bigwigs of Kolkata Police that this feeling of disaffection was expressed by the distinguished citizens.

When the idea of the distinguished persons regarding police forces is of the above character the general people's impression in this respect need not be elabrated upon. If during the last three decades somebody has to be primarily accused for this decline in the image of the police forces in the region the earlier left front government has to be held responsible. During the last three decades the police forces were never allowed to act in an impartial manner. The police was controlled by the CP(M) party office. Which police official will be entrusted with which responsibility was determined by the authorities of the Alimuddin

Street. Like other professions party allegiance was being given predominance. Consequently it was found that many worthless and unskilled police officers were installed in important positions by virtue of their intimacy with the party higher-ups. That apart the abominable action of injecting politics in the police service was also performed by the left front.

A kind of police officials took advantage of this narrow outlook of the left front government. They have simply appeased the party leaders and carried on their own illegal activities. The police have turned out to be the drawing rooms of the local party offices. The mastans who received indulgence from the party became the comrades-at-arms with the police. Not unlike the party cadres police has been utilised in political activities. Police also behaved like the party cadres. This corruption and politicisation of the police forces were opposed by honest and upright IPS officers like Najrul Islam who were consequently harassed and humiliated by the previous government.

Besides this politicisation there is the unbridled corruption of a class of police officials. Raising money like the tolabajs, taking bribes here and there - such malpractices have become their habits. Particularly when indigent people fall in distress and go to police stations for redress these dishonest police officials mulct money from them as rewards for insignificant services. For all these reasons people's confidence in police has gradually eroded. Day by day police has assumed the role of villains in the eyes of the ordinary citizens.

In the conference of June 8 the demand raised by the distinguished persons for altering the image of the police forces is highly justified. In the last three decades the image of the police almost reached the bottom; the immediate duty of the present government is to raise it up from that crevice. For this purpose the first thing that the government will have to do is to stop the politicisation of the police forces.

Outside the periphery of party obeisance police forces will have to operate impartially. Ordinary citizens will have to be convinced that the police forces will from now on take steps against the offenders without taking into account their polical pigment and the higher officers of Kolkata Police and regional police officers will have to mark out the corrupt officers and officials and arrange for their hard punishment.

It must be ensured that whenever the ordinary persons had occasions to visit the police stations they will receive appropriate remedies. The attitude to harass the poor and indigent visitors in an unjustified manner must be dispelled from the minds of the police officials. The officers and the officials must be taught the lesson of not surrendering before any poltical pressure. The mud which was slung in the uniform of the police during the last 30 years must be washed away at any cost.

30

IN THE CONTEXT OF EDUCATIONAL REFORM

After coming to power the new government has taken special initiatives in the matter of educational reform. There are two aspects of this reform: the all-round development of the standard of education in the region and recovery of the lost glory of Presidency College by turning it into a University. A few specialist committees have already been formed for this purpose and a special 'mentor group' has been set up with the internationally reputed educationists like the Nobel-wining economist Amartya Sen and Professor Sugata Basu of Harvard University.

What is more important is that the Chief Minister Mamata Banerjee is herself monitoring the whole matter of educational reform amidst her diverse administrative and political assignments. Naturally therefore in different circles this initiative of educational reform has generated ample inspiration. At the same time she has also created sufficient enthusiasm in the concerned circles by announcing payment of salaries of the teachers and the non-teaching staff on the first day of the month, provisional pension, assurance of the rapid payment of the arrears and announcements of different exemptions in the studies of the pupils and movements to schools and colleges. Witnessing this personal initiatives and efficiency of the chief minister Mamata Banerjee many ordinary people have got the impressions that something will happen this time. Like industry and health a big change will certainly come over the educational system of the country. The educational climate in schools, colleges and universities which has been vitiated so long by different kinds of politicking and the preponderance of mediocre elements will improve and students will not be cheated any longer after spending thousands of rupees, adequate recognition of talents will be received and taking all aspects into account the moribund circumtances in education will be enlivened once again.

Such hopes in today's West Bengal are not totally unfounded. The strongly positive outlook which Is noticed on behalf of the government in the matter of development of the standard of education is in fact generating such hopes in our minds. But the region is West Bengal and our Bengali nature is unalterable— That is why already in certain quarters questions have started being asked about some persons in the educational reform committee and their political identities. It is being said that most of her announcements will remain unimplemented. Everything is actually a kind of political gimmick. In the name of emancipating education from party dominance the ruling party Trinamool Congress is actually positing its own patrons in various places and committees. The purpose it is alleged is obvious. It is of course to replace the dominance of one party by that of another. What the leftists taught us throughout their 34 year's misrules that if you are a supporter of the leftists you are actually 'impartial' and an 'expert' in all matters while if, on the contrary, you are a supporter of Mamata Banerjee you are not only an enemy but also a 'polluted politician' from whom nothing can be expected. Singur, Darjeeling or the educational programmes of the Mamata Banerjee government- all are poohpoohed by the leftists in this manner.

But what is the benefit? Everyone knows that all these problems have been inherited from the previous government and each of them is extremely hard and complex which cannot be solved overnight. But Mamata Bannerjee and the members of her ministry have tried to tackle the problems on a wartime footing and progressed very much. Peace has returned to Darjeeling and deep expectations have been aroused in the minds of the Gorkhas regarding the development of the standard of living in the Hills. The peasants of Singur have been overwhelmed with joy at the prospects of return of their lands. Even in the static educational world of the region the movement of change has been noticed. Time alone can say that will happen ultimately and Mamata has succeeded or not in what matter. The earlier government could do nothing in the 34 years. Now when Mamata has started showing some achievements they have started politicking in the opposition bench. What the Education Committeee doing is not important in their eyes. They are more concerned with the question as to who among them are Trinamool and who are Naxals. But the real truth is that the comprehensive development of the standard of education is a multi dimensional issue for which is needed multi level planning and far reaching understanding and faith. The question of politics in this perspective is secondary. And then again the big question is whether that politics is positive or negative, whether it is an outcome of good will or whether it is controlled by the party directives?

During the 34 years of the CP(M) regime the sphere of education was converted in that negative politics controlled by the party directives. That is why they could perform nothing significant.

In the last lap of their regime they built up two incomplete Universities (Refound University at Barasat and the Gourbanga University) and declared a few startling pacakages for the candidates of the minorities and the Pichhre Barg. But there was a lack of well coordinated planning and experienced educationists for implementing those plans and programmes.

The inevitable effect was domination of CP(M), in schools, colleges and Universities. The major consideration was how many students were members of SFI, how many teachers and teaching activists registered their names in ABTA or WEBCUTA, how many CP(M) activists and how many oppositionists are there in the school committies and governing bodies. What should be the strategy to keep those opponets in control. Whether the principal was abiding by the instruction of the council or Alimuddin Street. All these became the chief concerns of studies and teaching. In every school or college there were appointed some activists of CP(M) through whom the information of the institution reached the local party office, the education cell and Alimuddin street in that order. In many cases the regular attendance of the principals in the party office became compulsory.

It is from this contagion of party politics that Mamata Banerjee has sought to save education at all levels. Certainly she is aware that the task is extremely difficult and for that is necessary a well thought out and integrated education policy. At the same time it is necessary

The whole history of Presidency College turns around its achievement as an undergraduate college. A few extraordinary teachers had been there. Their names are frequently heard in the lips of the intelligentsia who were the alumni of this institution. But the performance of Presidency College in the postgraduate level was not very remarkable. Because there had been a few unexceptionable teachers at the graduation level and because they had great commitment in the matter of teaching. The students of the Presidency College mastered their subjects thoroughly at the graduation level. In later days for postgraduate education they either went to the Science College or to the College Street campus of Calcutta University. Many students after graduating from Presidency College went to Delhi, Mumbai, Kanpur. Many students also went abroad. This was the culture of Presidency College.

At the graduation level a special tradition of the college was built up. A climate of teaching and learning was built up around a few teachers. These teachers have created a few generations. All these people have become successful in life. But unlike the illustrious ancestor of Prof. Sugata Basu no one has made so much sacrifices in the interest of the nation. In order to reconstruct Bengal and the place of Bengali institution in the world perspective that 'commitment' will be deemed absolutely necessary.

Derozio about whom I was talking a little earlier always used to enthuse his pupils to take part in debates with him. Not only that, he encouraged his students to argue against the side on which he was talking himself. In this way Derozio induced his students to form their own independent opinions and they also began to raise questions about their own household operations and that proved to be his own nemesis. By giving excuse of India's traditional ideals the man was driven out from history of the Presidency College.

The mindset of the Bengalees throws light on this history. But in order to construct something some other things have to be destroyed.

Futile egotism has to be dispensed with. Unless this is done man's internal strength cannot be awakened. Tolerance of the viewpoints of others has to be acquired. This is also a kind of self-exercise. Study of books can not give us this education. It has to be developed from one's own self. It has to be understood that a well-educated person is also a self-educated person. And an institution cannot also be built up if this ideal of self-education is done away with.

No institution can grow up overnight. The same law applies in the case of an educational institution. People of Britain, Europe and America know how to grow it up. We Indians are deficient in this. Bengalis are more inept in this respect. We are only interested in services which we have learnt from our European masters. But we did not learn from them the art of building up institutions. Just think for once how many institutions of international standard have been set up in independent India. Apart from that after the attainment of independence Presidency College retained its earlier glory till 1980 or 1985 or, in other words, for 30 to 40 years since 1947. This is only a consequence of the so called 'inertia of motion'. A wheel is moving it does not suddenly come to a stop. Its original motion keeps it moving for some time. Thereafter it slowly loses its motion.

In the sixties or seventies of the last century which type of students got admitted in Presidency College? Remember the rat race for studying medicine or engineering did not start as yet. Consequently the best students came to Presidency College with the intention of studying Physics or English or Economics. That picture began being totally altered since the eighties when the subjects of preference for the best students appeared to be medicine or eneineering.

The quality of raw materials has its inevitable impact on industry. If there is adulteration in raw materials an industrial establishment is compelled to increase its cost of production if the quality of the product is to be maintained at a high level. The same law is applicable to the sphere of education as well. An exceptionally good student can do well in the examination with little help from the college. But that is not possible for a less meritorious student. Therefore even for an exceptional teacher it is difficult to uphold the earlier standard of Presidency College. It would be an over-simplification if politics alone is accused for this phenomenon. An in-depth analysis and understanding will be called for on this account.

I have already commented that the Indians are not very adept in building institutions. In order to set up an institution self-interest has got to be sacrificed. Men who are prepared to undertake such sacrifices are extremely rare in our society. Although a few such men were noticed earlier as things stand today all those people have vanished altogether from the picture. Today's society runs after success and establishment. But the commitment or determination which is necessary for getting established or setting up institutions is normally absent. But we have to keep it in mind that without 'commitment' no solid achievement is ever possible.

The period when there were no such plethora of conferences witnessed researches of exceptionally high calibres in the city of Kolkata. But now everthing appear to be shallow and superficial. A few air travels, meetings with native and foreign guests and mutual back patting the foremost aim of the educational world seems to be to find out the 'summum bonum' of life among such events. This is the current craze and the index of intelligance lies in acting like so many veritable 'weather cocks'. Of course Derozio made a futile attempt to stand against the current craze and build up a new culture which, however did not fit in with our temperment. And that is why we tried every means fair and foul to drive him out from the precincts of the academic world.

32

RAMBLES ON PRESIDENCY UNIVERSITY- II

In the present perspective we have Presidency University. In the present age a university is known by the standards of its researches. The American universities are known by how many Nobel-winners are found to move about in their corridors. The recovery of the lost glory of Presidency College means nothing. Because all the grandeur of Presidency College was due to the extra ordinary standard of teaching of a few teachers at the undergraduate level. It would not be perhaps proper to say that although a few research centres were there those were actually centres of excellence.

As things stand today, Presidency College has started its journey as Presidency University. New paths and new objectives are necessary. In order to establish the institution on a novel basis' a totally novel attitude is necessary. The University has to be established with sincere efforts of highly expert students and teachers. This is an altogether different game.

The Presidency College of the undergraduate level and today's Presidency University are qualitatively different. An exceptionally good teacher may not necessarily be a good researcher. A famous researcher may not necessarily become a good teacher. In America a teacher who lost his job as a result of the judgement of the students was awarded Nobel Prize the next year of losing his job.

Presidency University has started its journey. People belonging to all the levels of the society, all the other universities of the region and the nation will have to come forward to its assistance. A university is not set up in a day. A university is the outcome of the efforts of many people. The Bengali i.e. Indian habit usually smacks of an escapist bent of mind. At the slighest difficulty we take to our heels. In order to set up an institution we must be brave enough to face all hazards and provide leadership. The mentor group will give the necessary directives and we the ordinary mortals will have to translate those directives into action.

The light of modern education came to India through the Hindu College which was then the pathbreaker. Today the perspective is different. 121 crores of people live today in India. Here only a few 'pockets of excellence' or 'Islands of excellence' will not serve the purpose.

Unless the supreme virtues of all persons are unified together it would not be possible to reach the apex of development. America has introduced such a system through which the paths for florination of the capabilities of even very ordinary persons have been opened. Of course we may have differences with the political system of America. But their dexterity in the matter of setting up institutions must be emulated by us. The ordinary students of our country go to America and attain excellence by virtue of these institutions. That knowledge of running an institution has to be mastered by us. The fittest persons must be given enough latitude, help and support and we must have confidence in their ability. An institution can be built up only in this way.

A question that automatically a rises in this context is whether there is a very serious difference between the academice qualifications of the authorities of the American universities and those in our countries? I do not think so. But successs is more conspicuous in those countries and less in our country. Where is the difference? My own idea is that the difference lies in the mind set. In those countries men have a dogged determination - inflexible decision, unflinching devotion to duty and the attitude of never escaping from the field of action. On the other hand we always have an escapist atttude. The sincerity that is urgently called for in the setting up of an institution is lacking in us.

The government has much responsibility in this context. The available human resources have to be utilised. Everybody must be involved in the matter. Along with the Presidency University all other universities should also be taken care of.

In a poverty-stricken country it is difficult to pay equal attention to all the matters. But if there is tenacity with honesty, if cleverness is replaced by intelligence there will of course be progress in the Bengali society. Unique human resources inside and lawns of green grasses outside, glittering coffee shops, the person engaged in clearing the road, the health of the swans swimming in the lakes putting our people to shame - these all constitute the surroundings of the universities of the foreign countries. Much time will be required to raise Presidency University to that standard. In the meanwhile we will have to keep faith in the mentor group. At the same time we must rightly perform our own respective duties. The vice-chancellor and his team should be given adequate time. The professors should be given their due respect. Let us make a united effort based on mutual trust and respect.

33

TECHNICAL EDUCATION IN THE SHAMBLES

Entrance examination and merely by securing 50% marks on an average in physics, chemistry and mathematics in the Higher Secondary Examination, one will be entitled to go in for studying engineering in this region. The new government which has been installed in power recently has adopted this novel decision. The Director of Technical Education under the Department of Higher Education, Sajal Dasgupta has disclosed this information. Sajal Babu's moot point is that for the last two years many seats have been remaining vacant in the private engineering colleges of this region. Last year about 650 seats remained vacant in 80 non-government colleges in the region. It is with a view to filling up these vacant seats that the new government has taken this decision. Of course Siddhartha Datta who is the chairman of the Central Selection Committee of the Joint Board of Engineering is wholly unaware of this 'novel' decision of the regional government. Nonetheless in the field of technical education this decision has assumed the form of the centre of gravity of a controversy inside the ruling party Trinamool Congress itself 'the criticism of this decision can be heard. The question that has arisen in this context is' how much this decision of the regional government is relevant and expedient?

What the regional government pleads is that since there are vacant seats in the non-governmental engineering colleges, this decision has been adopted. If this is the only reason for taking this decision by the government one must be forced to opine that this decision hardly helps in improving the standard of higher education. The standard of education can never be improved by somehow or other filling up the vacant seats in the private colleges. Rather the question that has arisen is what really is the purpose of the government-to improve the standard of education or fulfilling the business interest of the non-governmental colleges.

In the developed countries, however, the door of higher education is not open for everybody. In those countries higher education is available only on the basis of merit. Only those students who are above average get the opportunity for studying in colleges or universities. On the contrary in our case the door of higher education is open to everybody irrespective of the merit of the candidate. College or university degrees in our country are available to anybody and everybody. Consequently in our country the number of jobless people with degrees is also high. In developed countries it is difficult to topple the barriers of engineering and medical degrees.

In those countries in order to enter these specialised courses of study the students have to go through many screening processes. Previously in our country too there were many restrictions in getting the facility for studying medicine or engineering. Opportunities for studying these subjects were obtained only in cases of proven merit.

During the period of the left government, however, the door for higher education was opened to everybody especially in the sphere of engineering. The left front government opened numerous private engineering colleges in a misconceived effort to create a machinery for generating engineers in every household. This has led to an indiscriminate attitude towards quality. In many cases the judgment of merit is deficient. There has been a consequent decline in the standards of teaching and studying as well as the level of merits.

This time the decision of the new government leads to the apprehension that this will lead to further devaluation of standards. In the first place as a result of this decision the Joint entrance education will be bereft of all its earlier importance. The mediocre students who scored 50% marks on an average in physics, chemistry and mathematics in the Higher Secondary Education will be easily entitled to get admission in the engineering colleges. No one will go to judge whether they have the necessary talent for studying engineering. There will be an indiscriminate decline in the relative merits of the students in the colleges.

What is more important is that the number of jobless engineers in this region will be more inflated. The Director of Technical Education has observed that already the governments of Tamil Nadu, Karnataka and Orissa have legislated in order to facilitate the studies of engineering on the basis of the marks obtained in H.S. or equivalent examination. But only a little scrutiny will reveal that in those regions the thousands of students who pass out every year do not get any importance in the sphere of the job market.

The Technical Education Minister from this region Rabiranjan Chatterjee is a distinguished educationist who had also been the Dean of a university. It is expected that he has the ability to understand the harm that is done by allowing without adequate scrutiny all the mediocre students to study a course like engineering. Instead of being infatuated by the demands of the owners of the non-governmental engineering colleges if he really intends to improve the standard of technical education in the region, he will have to attach importance to the merits of the students aspiring to study engineering. Consequently he will have to desist from the step initiated by the regional government.

34

RIGMAROLE ON SCHOOL EDUCATION

Side by side with higher education, the regional government has taken initiative to improve the standard of school education in West Bengal. Already nine task forces have been constituted for the purpose of improving the standard of school education. In the list of priorities of these task forces there is the arrangement of training of the teachers of primary and secondary levels as per the direction of the centre, drawing up the syllabus in keeping with the national level and changing the text books, improvement of the school infrastructure, special monitoring in the midday meal project etc. It has also been decided that the chairman in charge of the task forces will sit in conference with the School Education Minister or the Departmental Secretary on the last Wednesdays of every month. It is no use denying the fact that the topics included in the list of priorities of the task forces are highly momentous. In order to improve the standard of school education adequate importance should be attached to all these matters. Looked at from this point of view the official decision for constituting nine task forces is of course thanksworthy.

It is not true that the picture of education in the region will improve only through the Presidency University or the development of the standard of higher education in West Bengal. In order to bring about a total improvement of the educational system in the region, work has to be started from the grassroot level of the educational system. If the grassroot level is defective, it will naturally have its impact on the sphere of higher education. In order to improve the talents and the standard of studies, attempts should be made from the school level. In case the roots of the tree are strong, it will naturally

What is more important is that the number of jobless engineers in this region will be more inflated. The Director of Technical Education has observed that already the governments of Tamil Nadu, Karnataka and Orissa have legislated in order to facilitate the studies of engineering on the basis of the marks obtained in H.S. or equivalent examination. But only a little scrutiny will reveal that in those regions the thousands of students who pass out every year do not get any importance in the sphere of the job market.

The Technical Education Minister from this region Rabiranjan Chatterjee is a distinguished educationist who had also been the Dean of a university. It is expected that he has the ability to understand the harm that is done by allowing without adequate scrutiny all the mediocre students to study a course like engineering. Instead of being infatuated by the demands of the owners of the non-governmental engineering colleges if he really intends to improve the standard of technical education in the region, he will have to attach importance to the merits of the students aspiring to study engineering. Consequently he will have to desist from the step initiated by the regional government.

34

RIGMAROLE ON SCHOOL EDUCATION

Side by side with higher education, the regional government has taken initiative to improve the standard of school education in West Bengal. Already nine task forces have been constituted for the purpose of improving the standard of school education. In the list of priorities of these task forces there is the arrangement of training of the teachers of primary and secondary levels as per the direction of the centre, drawing up the syllabus in keeping with the national level and changing the text books, improvement of the school infrastructure, special monitoring in the midday meal project etc. It has also been decided that the chairman in charge of the task forces will sit in conference with the School Education Minister or the Departmental Secretary on the last Wednesdays of every month. It is no use denying the fact that the topics included in the list of priorities of the task forces are highly momentous. In order to improve the standard of school education adequate importance should be attached to all these matters. Looked at from this point of view the official decision for constituting nine task forces is of course thanksworthy.

It is not true that the picture of education in the region will improve only through the Presidency University or the development of the standard of higher education in West Bengal. In order to bring about a total improvement of the educational system in the region, work has to be started from the grassroot level of the educational system. If the grassroot level is defective, it will naturally have its impact on the sphere of higher education. In order to improve the talents and the standard of studies, attempts should be made from the school level. In case the roots of the tree are strong, it will naturally

proliferate its branches. The educational field can be easily compared with it. If the school education is neglected, the thought of improving the higher education is an idle dream. It is a good angury that the new government is determined to avoid this pitfall. They have taken action to improve the standard of education right from the grassroot level. It may legitimately be expected that the benefits of this effort will be available in not too distant future.

During the last thirty years in this region side by side with higher education, much deterioration took place in school education. In the all India perspective in statistical terms this region went back to the last row. Like higher education in school education also the earlier leftist rulers went to the path of total politicisation The chief reason for the decline of school education was politicisation. During the leftist regime of the last three decades the service of a teacher would not be available unless one was a supporter or an activist of the ruling party. Instead of ability, party allegiance had become the chief point at issue.

School committees were organised by the stalwarts of CPI(M). The textbooks written by the authors who were close to the ruling party were prescribed in the schools. The teachers who remained under the umbrella of the ruling party paid greater attention to politics than the teaching of students. That apart by taking the injudicious step of abolishing English from the primary stage, the leftist rulers have totally destroyed the future of more than one generation. Throughout the last thirty years, the government was seen to adopt no effective initiative for the improvement of standard of school education. Rather as the inevitable result of the dilly dallying attitude of the government gradual decline has taken place in school education.

Very recently Bratya Basu has taken the charge of the Department of School Education along with his earlier charge of the Higher Education Department. In the improvement of the standard of school education, he should immediately pay attention to bringing about the improvement of school infrastructure. There are many schools in the region where the laboratories are deficient or the conditions of the libraries are unenviable. In many schools there are inadequate arrangements of the lavatories or the school buildings are dilapidated. The new school minister will have at least to make the schools fit for study purposes. He will have to keep watch that while coming to

study in the schools the students do not have to face any hazards. At the same time attention should be paid to the adequate training of the teachers. Importance should be attached to the problem of making the teachers aware of the world standard of teaching and practising those principles in their own life. The Education Minister should also take the initiative to bring about a change in the mindsets of the teachers. He must also be alert that the school teachers are freed from the mentality of half-hearted teaching in the school and private tuition outside. Before all these attempts should be made to stop the conversion of the schools into political training centres. Whichever party attempts to indulge in such malpractices, should be ruthlessly suppressed. Attention should be paid to the fact that the service of the school teacher must be based on worthiness and merit. No political identity should be given importance in this mattter.

The way the standard of school education has declined during the last thirty years indicate that it is not possible to rescue school education within one or two months. The task is difficult as well as time-consuming. Nor is it a fact that this will not involve direct confrontation with many vested interests. Nonetheless the government and the school education minister will have to tackle these obstacles in a determined manner. If these tasks are performed with adequate sincerity, benefits will definitely be available in future.

35

EDUCATIONAL CONUNDRUM

What is the means to bring about excellence in education? This question is being occasionally heard here and there in 'altered' West Bengal. The preparation for newly building the Presidency University is patently visible. A special committee has been constituted to bring about reforms in higher education. Different projects or proposals for bringing about changes in secondary or higher secondary education are also floating in air. Of course primary education is outside the periphery of discussion even now, perhaps somewhat forgotten. Nonetheless, the discussion about education as in such a stagnant society like West Bengal is not significant. The talent resources of this region is historical-perhaps the foremost ability of this region. but during the last few decades there has been a terrible decline in such resources. Therefore if we really wait to turn round, our first duty will be to bring about improvement in education which means education at all levels. If we want to improve the economic condition of West Bengal rapid reform of higher education is really necessary. Looked at from that point of view the importance accorded to colleges and universities is highly important. But an unpleasant truth should be remembered at the very beginning.

It would have been nice if all the colleges and universities could be upgraded to a sufficiently high level but actually it is difficult, practically impossible. At the very initial stage of the Presidency University one truth has come out in bold relief. Without the arrangememt for special financial grants, it would be difficult to attract teachers or researchers of sufficiently high levels to this university.

Just as it is true that finance is not the only attraction to them it is also no less true that it is difficult to attract them without a minimum financial incentive. Just because only teachers of international levels are relevant here the yardstick of international levels of salaries and allowances cannot be forgotten within the conventional structure of government colleges and universities. That is why special arrangements are necessary. It is for this reason that the project for improving all the educational institutions in unison is unrealistic. The theory of 'communistic' equality is invalid in higher education.

The same words are applicable in the case of education at the secondary levels. In comparison to higher education a greater number of 'centres of excellence' is necessary to build up at the school level and it is also possible. But this is a question of numbers, the real truth remains unaltered thereby. All the schools cannot be developed to the same extent. Not that finance is the only scarce factor. Even if adequate finance is available an adequate number of teachers of high standard are not available.Therefore in this sphere also a few ideal educational institutions need be set up.

In the British period the district schools were built up for this purpose. In many cases those were recognised as 'centres of excellence'. Ethically we can very well think of bringing about this structure. If possible in large districts more than one ideal school can be built up and if the number of districts are increased naturally the number of schools can be increased. In many cases for the district schools houses and primary infrastructures need not be built up afresh.

In quite a few schools these are already there and certain schools are really developed so far as standard of teaching is concerned. In other words, improvement in education need not start from zero.

What is necessary is to keep excellence as the target. Once the target is fixed finding out the route becomes easy.

36

REMOVING HURDLES FROM INDUSTRY

Chief Minister Mamata Banerjee knows it well that only help from the national government will not mitigate the economic problems of West Bengal. That is why she reminded a few days ago that the region must be financially self-reliant. It must draw up the guidelines for standing on its own feet. With that purpose in view collection of fiscal revenues must be increased and large capital and heavy industries must be brought to the region at an early date. In order to facilitate the path of industrialisation she has given direction to the Industries Minister Partha Chatterjee that as early as possible the unfinished industrial projects should be disentangled. Or, in other words, these should be freed from the regulations of red-tapism. When Manmohan Singh visited Kolkata Mamata took his advice regarding the manner in which economic revitalisation of West Bengal can be brought about and which are the fields where industrial development can take place.

A lawsuit is hanging on over the Singur problem. The position of the new government regarding acquisition can not be violated. Violation of the interests of the peasants should not be allowed. This does not mean that Mamata does not want industry. Actually, however, she is in favour of industrialisation and her objective is to facilitate the path of establishment of new industries in this region.

Following the directions of the chief minister attempts have been made to overcome complexities in the case of applications for new industries and very soon 'one window system' is going to be introduced. Said the Industries Minister, 'Previously, for the purpose of getting recommendations of new industries 99 forms were required to be filled up. Indian Chamber of Commerce was given the responsibility for simplifying this process. Thereafter the number of forms was reduced to 35. But the chief minister was not pleased even then. Right now the number of forms has been reduced to 15. From this fact it is obvious that Mamata is now giving priority to the matter of industrialisation.

Quite a few new decisions are being adopted by her so that the aspect of industrialisation is not neglected.

The Managing Director of West Bengal Industrial Development Corporation, Nandini Chakravarti opined that we are not asking the entrepreneurs to invest in industry only because a new government has taken over in West Bengal. Rather such an infrastructure is being sought to be built up by the government, so that an industrialist may be enthused to undertake investment. If years after years were required to get licences for industries, if in order to submit the application it was seen the same information was required to be written for pages after pages the investor will naturally become disheartened. The 15-page application form which has been drawn up at present includes the value-added tax also. If that portion is ommitted total number of pages in the letter of intent will be 13.

From the Industries Department sources, it has been known that this letter of intent can be submitted on-line. After one week it will be known in what position it is lying.

Although new acquisition of land is postponed for the time being the government is paying attention to the fact that there is no scarcity of land for new industry. There are 35 industrial parks under the WBIDC for each of which the Industries Department has already prepared a database. How much land is unused even now and what are the infrastructural facilities- evey such thing is clear now. Consequently those who will come to build up industries will get the facilities for selecting the lands according to their own choice.

So that licences for industry can be issued promptly the Industries Department has built up a core committee with the representatives of Departments of Finance, Urban Development, Agriculture, Irrigation, Small Industries, Power, Environment and Fisheries. Frequent meetings of this committee are held. Consequently the opinions of different departments regarding a project are promptly being known at present.

In certain cases the approval of the national government is also known for the industrial projects of the region. In quite a few cases that licence is given on-line by the Centre. Attempts are being made so that different projects of the region can get the letters of approval of different departments of the Centre within seven days. The chief minister has informed that for this purpose she will herself consult the national government. Apart from that the national Commerce ministry has adopted a new project to facilitate the application process of the entrepreneurs with INFOSIS. This attempt is called 'Pay One, Apply One'. In a particular line of industry application fee will be given only for once. On that basis the letters of approval of all the departments will be available.

As per the directives of the chief minister, on the one hand, investment process is being simplified and on the other new investments are showing rays of hopes.

The chief minister, Mamata Bannerjee has recently inaugurated the Bengal Intelligence Park of Purnendu Chatterjee in Sector-5 of Salt Lake. For that ITI knowledge based project conceived by Purnendubabu 200 workers will be given training. There had been a discussion between Purnendubabu and Mamata Banerjee. The Industries Minister Partha Chatterjee has informed that with a view to building up the Poly Park in Haldia Purnendu Chatterjee and Associates have already invested one thousand crores of rupees. In future further 4,500 crores of rupees will be invested.

Previosly there was some complexity regarding the industrial corporation at Shalbani of Sajjan Jindal. Because there permission was not taken regarding the ceiling of land. Of course Mamata has explained that not that the project will not be implemented because it was started in the regime of Buddhadev Bhattacharya. She wants to rectify the deficiencies in the case of those projects which were not implemented earlier due to administrative failures. Right now the project of the Jindals are free from all complexities. Prathababu wants to emphasise that instead of judging the political colour of the entrepreneurs all the projects have been examined impartially. Care is taken of the fact so that the projects do not go against the interests of the peasants.

Its effects are already at hand. Y.K. Modi has already invested one thousand crores of rupees. In Barasat Rs. 500 crores have been invested in a cloth factory. In Domjir golden ornaments and diamond hub has been set up. In Kharagpur Tractor India is engaged in setting up a corporation for manufacturing machinery and component parts. In Sankrail a foundry hub is being set up. Foundry Park Associtio n is also setting up a hub at Howrah's Panihati. Prasun Mukherjee of Universal Success submitted a few projects for Nayachar and recently he had a conference with Partha Chatterjee over those projects.

Mamata Bannerjee has given the green signal to those projects, because these projects are ecofriendly (just what Mamata wanted). Following the demands of the regional government Pasunbabu's organisation has submitted the Financial Disclosure Report. Parthababu is very much pleased at the receipt of this report. In the meanwhile Partha Chatterjee had a meeting with Mukesh Ambani. The latter has shown interest in building up a food processing industry park. Anil Ambani also is investing capital in animation industry in this region. Mukesh Ambani, Anil Ambani and Sajjan Jindal are interesed in having meetings with chief minister Mamata Bannerjee. A schedule has also been prepared for this purpose. Mamata wants to be elected to the Vidhan Sabha. Besides that, the chief minister is also giving priority on generation of power so that there may not be any deficit 'of power in industry. Every Friday she is meeting in conference with the Industries Minister, Finance Minister and the Power Minister where each of the projects are being reviewed in detail.

PART- II

(SEPTEMBER-DECEMBER 2011)

37

HAVEN OF INVESTMENT IS WEST BENGAL

The regional government claims that West Bengal is going to be the new haven for investment. Using the international trade fair in New Delhi this message was given by the chief minister Mamata Banerjee.

This is the first time that in the current trade fair West Bengal has become a partner 'region'. Utilising that opportunity she explained the current circumstances of the region before the circle of industrialists and the dignitaries of different nations and gave the assurance for setting up industries. She also threw light before the industrialists on the successes of her own government during the last six months and demarcated the specific spheres of investment. Development of food processing, agricultural marketing, health education and tourism were specifically stressed in a seminar at Pragati Maidan entitled 'Rising Bengal' and Mamata commented that in our region there are various spheres where there are opportunities for investment. We earnestly desire that captains of industry should come forward to invest in these areas. Already durng the last six months the region has received the assuraance of 56,000 crores of rupees.

The Finance Minister of the region Amit Mitra commented that the fruits of the initiatives of the regional government have already started being available. Quite a few foreign organisations, like Mitsubishi have shown interest in investment. Already they have come forward to set up a manufacturing unit in the region.

The chief minister has also issued a few declarations necessary for industrial development. The non-resident industrialist Prasun

Mukherjee appealed to her that for the puroose of development project in Nayachar island it is extremely necessary to establish communication with the maintanance through the building of a bridge. In reply Mamata assured that this communication will be set up through the railways. Recently the regional Industries Minister Partha Chatterjee had a discussion with the national minister Jayanti Natarajan regarding the licences relating to Nayachar. Jayanti informed that the matter would be settled very soon.

Mamata has all along highlighted the negative attitude of the industrial circles which have been created in West Bengal during the leftist rule of 34 years. She now opined that there is now a sincere effort on the part of the regional government to come out of this negative mindset. In her words we are imploring all the countries like America, Britain, Germany, China to invest capital in West Bengal. We have cheap labour here. An auxiliary atmosphere for industrial development has been created here.

It has to be remembered that West Bengal is the gateway to Bangladesh, Nepal and Bhutan. We have common boundaries with many regions in the north-east. Consequently in case of investment in our region the markets for so many nations can be captured. She also informed that in order to attract investment Rising Bengal Summit will be held on 6-11 January in the regions adjacent to New Delhi. Industrialists like Prasun Mukherjee, Sanjay Budhia and Y.K. Modi admitted that the climate of investment i.e. the overall circumstances in the region are gradually changing. The national Commerce Minister Ananda Sharma advised that the infrastructural development in the region should be given topmost priority. He informed that in the near future ASEAN Industrial Summit will be held in West Bengal.

In the case of the region land acquisition is a highly sensitive matter. That is why Mamata recently assured the industrialists to the effect that the region has set up land banks. There are also land-maps. If the industrialists so desire they can also themselves acquire land. In case industry is required to be set up availability of land will be no problem. At the same time the chief minister informed the industrialists that in order to avoid all kinds of red-tapism the government has introduced 'single window' arrangement for the industrial system.

38

WHO ARE THE GREATER LEFTISTS?

Who are the greater leftists? CP(M) - CPI or, the Trinamool Congress? In the question of national approval in foreign investment in retail trade the equivalent opposition of the two warring rivals recently highlighted this vital question. After petrol came the question of foreign investment in retail trade and there was the paradoxical situation that TMC criticised the national government by attuning their utterances with the opponents. And going to do that the TMC MPs actually embarked in a competition with the leftists.

On November 22, in the meeting of the national cabinet the MPs of the four leftist parties became vocal in the Parliament in protest against foreign direct investment of 51% in retail trade. On November 25, TMC joined in that protest. In the recent past probably this type of reaction was noticed for the first time. Of course the Trinamool MPs did not raise a hue and cry by coming down to the well unlike the leftists. Since they were the partners of the leftist government they showed restraint in this manner. But there was no difference in their language of opposition to the national government.

Side by side with the leftists as well as TMC all the opposition parties including BJP and even the other partner of the national government DMK also became vocal in the Parliament. In both the chambers of the Parliament along with the opponents the two partners of the government raised a hue and cry and the proceedings of the meeting were obstructed. In the Rajyasabha a few leftists and BJP MPs tore down the statement of the national Commerce Minister Ananda Sharma over the decision of the national cabinet.

The sessions of both the chambers of the Parliament were progressed. Consequently for four days at a stretch both the chambers of the Parliament remained virtually paralysed.

But the matter did not end here. The leftist, TMC and BJP leaders gave the indication that in future also much unrest may be created in the Parliarent. BJP and the leftists wanted to bring prorogue proposal in this matter in the Parliament. But in the Loksabha the leader of TMC, the state Minister of Health. Sudip Banerjee said, since we are partners of the national government, owing to the parliamentary obligations we cannot bring prorogue proposals. But strategically we will oppose it. He made reference to the question of the rise in oil price and commented that TMC has already shown in the recent past to what extent opposition can be drawn to the national government.

The leftist parties have all along opposed the entry of foreign investment in retail trade. Their rationale is that this will result in the exploitation of the country's peasants, agricultural labourers and small traders. Now the TMC is also raising their voice of protest in the same strain and arguing that the national government can hardly adopt any such policy which can cast a negative influence on the livelihoods of the peasants, small traders and agricultural labourers. Recently TMC raised this issue in the Loksabha as well. Their contention is that this decision of the Centre will engulf the small peasants and the small shopkeepers. Apart from that the foreign investors will at first purchase commodities from the peasants with extra money and keep it in storage.

The peasants will be enthused to produce more but in the next year the situation will become such that they will be unable to sell their produce. Whereupon they will be compelled to sell their produce at lower prices. In this way, TMC apprehends, new avenues of peasant suicides will be opened up. This is the reason of their objection. DMK is also opposing the decision of the national government in the same strain.

The CP(M) leader Basudev Acharya commented that all the opponent parties along with the partners of UPA like TMC and DMK were opposing the decision of the national government. Basudev and the CPI leader Gurudas Dasgupta informed that they would bring prorogue proposal against the decision of the national government. Gurudas recently talked with Sudip in this matter. But Sudip explained to him the limitations of the TMC.

BJP also threatened to bring prorogue proposal against this issue. Later a leader of the party Murali Manohar Joshi informed that the regions under the administration of BJP are advised that they should not implement this policy of the national government. The regions under Congress administration should also walk along the same avenue.

But the Parliamentry Affairs Minister Paban Banshal commented that a prorogue proposal of BJP regarding the recovery of black money had already been adopted. In the same session of the Parliament prorogue proposals cannot be raised more than once.

When asked to comment about the opposition of TMC - DMK he said that all the political parties have the right to express their own opinion.

Written objections were submitted by TMC and DMK. Questions were raised by Congress leaders like the Ministers like Jairam Ramesh and A.K. Anthony. The TMC leader and the Railways Minister Dinesh Trivedi walked out on this occasion from the meeting of the cabinet. Nonetheless the Manmohan Ministry disregarded that opposition and managed to secure the reco ommendation for foreign investment in retail trade of more than one brand of commodities. It is presumed that owing to quite a few economic and political obligations the national cabinet had to ignore the opinions of the partner parties.

The principal reason is of course to alter the total image of the national government. The Prime Minister Manmohan Singh and the Finance Minister Pranab Mukherjee had the responsibility to change the impression that the national government had moved away from the path of economic reform while going to tackle the problem of corruption in public life. They had also the resposibility to restore the confidence of the investors and the industrial circles. When on the one hand the external value of rupee is descending at a terrific rate and there is a crash in the stock market that resposibility has been much more magnified. Yesterday's decision had its impact on today's stock market. The sensex has come down as a whole this day also. But the share prices in the organisations of retail trade of the merchandise of more than one brand like Shoppers Stop, Pantaloons, Bishal and Trent have gone up.

The Manmohan Government is presupposing that the way foreign investment is mostly being attracted to America owing to the European crisis a few portions of it will of course this time be diverted to India. Those foreign investors who were so far withdrawing their capital from the Indian market will regain their confidence after watching the positive outlook of the national government. The Finance Ministry has the impression that this will revitalise the 'real estate' sector. Because those organisations who in view of the recession held up their programmes for building maills or shopping complexes will again be interested in launching new programmes.

It is understood that Pranababu explained to the Railways Minister that West Bengal had little chances of any harm at this occurrence. Because the West Bengal Government has already taken into account the interests of the small traders and peasants and consequently has the likelihood of imposing restrictions on the retail organisations in the region. That condition has already been retained. But TMC cannot obstruct the process if others regions presume that they will be benefited as a result. Congress leaders are saying that TMC did not extend this time their resistance to the same extent which they did at the time of enacting the land bill or hiking the prices of petrol products. They did not this time totally obstruct the path of taking decisions.

The Governor of the Reserve Bank,. D.Subbarao today expressed the hope that this decision of the national cabinet will result in controlling the rise in prices. Because there will be improvement in the system of supply of the agricultural products. So long among the farmers and the buyers the middle men derived the greatest benefit. The peasants received less prices for the agricultural products and the buyers used to pay higher prices. In the organised retail trade the peasants also will receive higher prices than previously, the buyers also will receive products at less prices. What is more important is that investment will be made in the country in the correct method.

As per the estimate of the national Commerce Minister, Ananda Sharma in case of foreign investment in retail trade one crore of new jobs will be created in 3 years. As per the government estimates 40 lakhs of jobs will be created in the retail trade centres and the rest in the supplies and transport sectors.

The industries and Commerce Minister Ananda Sharma recently

informed the journalists that in case any region wants that, it can withhold the permission of retail trade to any multinational corporation. Taking into consideration the probable objection of Mamata Banerjee's West Bengal as well as other regions, this matter has been kept in the national - regional concurrent list. But Ananda Sharma expected that any progressive region will definitely welcome foreign investment in retail trade in its own area. Previously in Kolkata and recently in the trade fair Ananda Sharma discussed this issue with Mamata Banerjee.

The topmost level of the Manmohan Government points out that in future the national government wants to invite foreign investment also in the sphere of civil aviation.

Before that it was necessary to give the information that the Manmohan Government is committed in the reform programme of the second phase.

39

KISHENJI'S DEATH AND THEREAFTER

The topmost Maoist leader, Mallajula Koteshwar Rao alias Kishenji has been killed recently in a conflict with the Cobra forces in the Burishole forest in the Jambani area of West Medinipur. Recently the curtain has dropped over the dramatic life of this character enshrouded in mystery who remained hidden from public sight for thirty years. For this long period Kishenji had been the reason for head ache to the police and administration in Andhra Pradesh, Chhattisgarh, M.P., Orissa, Jharkhand, West Bengal and Bihar.

In the past also even by conducting repeated enquiries the police and the allied forces found no traces of Kishenji. Every time in the last moment he threw dust in the eyes of the police and allied forces. On behalf of the administration the price of this Maoist leader was fixed at Rs. 35 Lakhs. At last Kishenji failed to escape from the clutches of the Cobra forces and his bullet-shot body was recovered in the Burishole forest.

Another Maoist guerilla leader Suchitra Mahato was known to be wounded in conflict with the Cobra forces. Undoubtedly this incident was a great success for the allied forces. Such a great success against the Maoists was never achieved in any previous campaign.

Although in the meanwhile some allegations were levelled from some quarters around the death of Kishenji. It has been alleged that this death did not occur as a result of military action. He was actually captured by the Cobra forces. He was later killed in a mock conflict.

Kishenji's mother herself brought this allegation. The real

40

GREATER EMPHASIS SHOULD BE PAID TO POWER SECTOR

The music of Durgapuja was still ringing in the air when the citizens of the region fell in the clutches of severe loadshedding. During the last few days, the amount of shortfalls in both the WBSEB and CESC areas have been abnormally increased. Of course two days ago since the demand for power in the region was much less, the amount of loadshedding was somewhat less. Nonetheless the authorities of the regional Power Department could not utter any words of hopes regarding the improvement of the circumstances. Rather the words they have uttered caused sufficient apprehension. The authorities of the Power Department are saying that on the occasion of Dipavali, the entire region of West Bengal may suffer from a power crisis. For this unbalanced position of power the Power Department is accusing the scarcity of coal as the chief reason. The amount of coal stored in the unit of Power Development Corporation has reached the rockbottom level. Coal for one or two days have been stored in Kolaghat, Bakreswar, Bandel and Sagardighi. It is obvious that on the working days if the demand for power is increased the region will again face disaster.

Under the circumstances neither the Power Minister Manish Gupta nor the authorities of the Power Department could utter any words of hopes. It has been announced in newspapers that due to the fact that a large amount of finance remaining unpaid by the regional government coal supplying organisations are refusing to supply coal. As a result, the stock of coal has dwindled and a critical situation has arisen.

Of course the power Minister Manish Gupta has four days ago gave the assurance of 60 crores of rupees to Eastern Coalfields Limited. Even after two days, it was announced in newspapers that finance was not paid so far. The authorities of the Power Development Corporation presume that even if that finance is deposited within one or two days, there will be little improvement in the circumstances. They are saying that 3 days ago the Power Development Corporation received 16 rakes of coal according to demand. But on the next day it was again reduced. Simultaneously with it, problems have been multiplied for the reason that power generating centres have not been modernised in due period at Kolaghat, Bakreswar and Bandel.

The power sector has a special role in the development and industrialisation of the region. Particularly there is an intimate nexus between Power and industrialisation. That is why in cases the government wants to doncern itself with development and industrialisation, it must also speculate separately about the sphere of power with special emphasis on it. With a view to developing the sphere of power, careful steps have to be taken on the basis of an emergency.

Although after being installed into the saddle, the new government started thinking deeply with various other sectors. No special consideration has still now been made about the power sector. It has also not been known whether the government has any special programme about the power sector. After the new government came to the saddle for the first three months, the Power Department was in the hands of the chief Minister Ms. Mamata Banerjee. Thereafter the charge of that department was given to Manish Gupta. After assuming the charge of the Power Department, Manish Gupta has been confronted with this severe problem of loadshedding.

At the root of the present power crisis, the chief reason is the dwindling of the supply of coal and its stock. The supply and stock of coal did not take place in one day. For a pretty long time, the crisis was deepening. Since that has taken the final shape everybody has now become alerted. After coming to the saddle, the new government attached adequate importance to the power sector from the very beginning, identified the specific problems in different areas in a detailed manner. This problem originating from the supply of coal could never escape their notice and they also could find adequate time for tackling the problems in a befitting manner. And the Power Minister also could not have to behave in a directionless manner after the problem assumed an acute shape.

Apart from that there is also the problem of lack of timely modernisation of the power generating centres in Kolaghat, Bakreswar and Bandel. The responsibility for not modernising these plants mostly belongs to the previous leftist government organised by CPI(M). It was they who damaged the power generating centres by accepting cutmoney and placing orders for installing machinery of poor qualities. It was in their period that the burden of debt increased due to failure in timely payment of money to coal supplying agencies.

Still then the present government will have to understand that in the circumstances, they should not wash their hands only after criticizing and accusing their predecessors. It should appreciate which sector should receive priority and which action should he performed first with utmost urgency. The government would have to draw up its programmes accordingly. In case there is no improvement in the power sector, no industrial organisation will ever look up at the face of this region. After realising this truth, priority should be accorded by the Power Minister and the top leaders of the regional government to the power sector. Right steps should be adopted in the matter of development of the standards of the power generating centres.

41

MORE ABOUT POWER SECTOR

The power Department of the region has made an understanding for receiving coal from Eastern Coalfields Limited (ECL) on the condition of not repaying the cess in an attempt to tackle the power crisis of the region. In a meeting with the ECL authorities, the Power Minister of the region Manish Gupta himself has entered into this understanding. It has been known from the Chief Minister's secretariat that before about seven days, the Power Minister Manish Babu sat in a conference with the Managing Director of ECL regarding the supply of coal. The Managing Director of ECL proposed to the Power Minister that since the regional government is failing to meet the price of coal, it should give up the claim to the money to be obtained as cess from the ECL. In exchange for that money, ECL will keep the supply of coal at the normal level. The Power Minister eagerly welcomed this proposal of ECL. He informed the ECL that on the basis of this understanding, they should continue to send coal to the regional government. It was then that the principle of receiving coal in exchange for cess was finalised.

Before allowing the cess to remain unpaid, the Power Minister never previously had any discussion with either the Finance Minister or any senior Officer of the Power Department. Even in the meeting where the Power Minister adopted this decision, no representative of the Finance Minister was present. It was by keeping the Finance Minister in the dark that the Power Minister took a unilateral decision in such an important matter. Naturally a controversy has been created over this decision of the Power Minister. The question has arisen whether the Power Minister can unilaterally adopt such a decision by actually sidetracking the Finance Department?

The question of collecting the cess is connected with the principle of collecting the revenues of the region. It is the jurisdiction of only the Finance Department to adopt any decision regarding the collection of revenues. In case the other departments have any pertinent point to suggest in this matter, they can inform the Finance Minister. But no decision can be independently adopted by any department. Looking at that point of view, the unilateral decision that the Finance Minister has adopted regarding the non-payment of cess by ECL contravenes the official regulations. Of course there is plausibility in the argument of the Power Department that there is no finance in their hands. The purpose of allowing the ECL not to pay the cess is that they will enable the Power Department to receive coal. There is no way to deny the fact that in this region crisis has appeared in the power sector due to the shortfall in the supply of coal.

In this case, owing to lack of finance, the Power Department is hamstrung. Consequently the Power Department could send the proposal for cancelling the cess to the Finance Department. Instead this unilateral decision by the Finance Department will strike at the root of coordination inside the government. If by taking the Power Department as a precedent, other departments *also* continue to take similar decisions the coordination between the government will be destroyed and consequently the government *will* have to face further financial difficulties.

This decision of the Power Department will result in a financial crisis of great magnitude for the regional government. The annual earning of the regional government on account of cess of coal is Rs. 110 crores. Cancelling the cess means that this huge income will be cut down.

Naturally the question will arise as to how the regional government will make up this deficit. The estimate received from the Chief Minister's secretariat reveals that this decision will make the financial crisis of the region more complex.

It has been known that right now the total monthly loss of the power generation and distribution company is Rs.225 crores. As a result of increase of contingency expenditures, very *soon* it will exceed the figure of Rs. 260 crores. At the same time Rs. 110 crores to be received as cess from the ECL will have to be adjusted with the price of coal. With that will be added the monthly payment of power tariff of Rs. 40 crores by the power department to the regional government and Rs. 40 crores as the interest of the credit taken from the government. Even if this Rs. 190 crores is kept aside, every month the deficit amounts to Rs. 70 crores. Apart from that the amount of finance which used to be deposited in the exchequer as being the cess from ECL will also be cut down. The result is that the quantum of liquid finance which will be daily required for running the government will fall short.

Of course, the power minister did not take into account the future possibilities before adopting this unilateral decision. In case he did premeditate on such vital matters, he would certainly be inhibited from making hurry in taking such a crucial decision. Now he is required to preview the future possibilities and enter into a conference with the finance department in order to find out a feasible solution of the likely future pitfalls. Otherwise the entire region will have to bear the brunt of his indiscretionary and myopic decision.

42

MORE ON SCHOOL EDUCATION

The regional government has taken the decision that following the Right to Education Act, upto Class VIII no student should be detained in the same class. Two days ago in the conference of the regional cabinet, this decision has been unanimously adopted. After the meeting of the cabinet, this decision of the regional government has been announced by the Industries and Commerce Minister Partha Chatterjee. It was clear from the declaration of Partha Chattarjee that upto class VIII in secondary schools, the matter of success or failure will not remain any further.

It was in the period of the left front that the system of success or failure at the primary stage was given the go-bye. It was from the educational year 1983-84 that decision to abolish the system of success or failure was made effective at the primary stage. Recently going to announce the new decision at the meeting of the regional cabinet, the Industries Minister has declared that in order to assess the learning of the students in the classes, the system of evaluation will be introduced. Otherwise the weaknesses of the students could not be identified.

There was a time when by abolishing the system of success or failure at the primary stage, the left front government was in the throes of a severe criticism. A section of the distinguished educationists of the region still holds the opinion that by abolishing the system of success or failure at the primary stage, the earlier government under the leadership of CPI(M) has actually spoiled the future of the boys and girls. It can be easily presupposed that the new government by adopting the decision of abolishing the system of success or failure upto class VIII in secondary schools, a controversy will again appear. Not unlike the former left front government, the new government will have to face adverse criticism from many quarters.

Two days ago after declaring this decision in the meeting of the regional cabinet, a controversy has started. No matter how emphatically the Industries Minister asserted that in order to assess the learning of the students in the classes, there will be a system of evaluation most of the teachers' organisations do not agree to accept the new decision. Their moot point is that if upto class VIII the system of success or failure is replaced by the grading system this will ultimately cause harm to education at the secondary school. Even Professor Sunanda sanyal who has been appointed as the chairman of the syllabus committee constituted by the School Education Department has disagreed to see eye to eye with this decision of the new government, in this context the observation of the regional Education Minister Bratya Basu is noteworthy. When asked to comment on the why this decision was adopted by the regional cabinet the Education Minister replied: Ask the Chief Minister. In other words the Education Minister was reluctant to enter into any such debate or discussion.

It cannot be totally denied that there are a few practical disadvantages in abolishing the method of success or failure till class VIII in secondary schools. In the first place the students of class VIII have to appear in the secondary examination after two years. Looked at from this point of view, if there is no longer the method of success or failure till class VIII, the necessary mindset for appearing in the secondary examination lord not grow up among the students. That apart, whether the students have been fit for studies in the secondary level, cannot be known through the process of winnowing any further. At the same time the teachers' organisations are also telling of another possible bad effect of abolishing the system of success or failure upto class VIII. They are saying that as a result of this questionable decision, the students themselves will fail to be in a position to appreciate what the exact level of depth of their learning is. Guardians also will fail to gauge the exact extent of the learning of their children. Right before the secondary examination when they will be confronted with this issue they will simply have no time to rectify the drawbacks of their children. None of these arguments can in fact be refuted easily.

Education in fact is a highly sensitive issue. On the adoption of a correct decision depends the future of the next few generations. If in the sphere of education a sudden decision is adopted without considering the pros and cons, it may result in considerable harm to the next generations.

The previous left front government abolished the system of learning English in the primary stage and thus caused harm to the future of quite a number of generations. If not unlike the last leftist government, the new government also fails to consider the pros and cons before taking an unwise decision, it will be a reason for apprehension from the point of view of the following generations.

Before adopting the momentous decision of abolishing the system of success and failure, this government ought to have entered into discussions with different teachers organisations and educationists. But the present government did not care to do that. Just as during the regime of the left front there was a noticeable tendency to impose a decision from above, the new government also displayed a comparable tendency at the time of introducting the decision to abolish the system of success or failure till class VIII in secondary schools.

Education Minister Bratya Basu said in Delhi that there is no truth in any such possibility. After the Education Minister said such words, it would be perfectly justified if the regional government was wise enough to enter into a discussion with the distinguished teachers and teaching organisations before taking a praiseworthy and pragmatic decision in this matter. The regional government can ill afford to forget that the future of a few following generations is inextricably intertwined with this single decision. That is why any puerile shortsightedness or indiscretion does not fit in well with its honest intentions.

43

AGRICULTURAL CRISIS CONTINUES

The Food Minister of West Bengal Jyoti Priya Mallik has claimed after the change of government that paddy worth one hundred crores of rupees has been purchased. This claim of his is likely to generate the hope in the public psyche that the peasants have been really benefited as a result of this official initiative. But the real truth is otherwise. Whatever be the claim of the government, the peasants have not yet received relief from the hands of the middlemen. They are in fact remaining in the same darkness they had been in the previous regime. But the middlemen are making huge profits like in the earlier days. In the previous leftist regime there was acute grievance among the peasants about the purchase of paddy at support prices. During the regime of the leftist government, paddy used to be purchased through cooperatives at the head of which there were mostly the CPI(M) leaders. In collusion with the owners of mills, little quantities of paddy used to be purchased from the peasants and the rest amount used to be purchased from the middlemen. Consequently the market of paddy could never be revived in an effective manner. Instead of going through the cooperatives, the new government has embarked in directly purchasing paddy through owners of mills at support prices. But paradoxically, this decision of the new government has resulted in deepening further the crisis of the government.

The bands of middlemen who are appointed by the mill-owners and by taking advantage of the poverty of the peasants they are purchasing paddy at the rate of Rs. 530/- to Rs. 540/-. When that paddy enters the mills, its price becomes Rs. 648/- per sack. It is actually the owners of the mills who are enjoying the major portion of the profits. The peasants observe that just in the same way in which potato used to be purchased at support prices in the leftist regime through the middlemen, the new government is also throttling the peasants in almost the same manner.

At the same time in a different news item, it was seen that in Hooghly district middlemen are purchasing vegetables from the peasants at lower prices and selling those at exorbitant prices. In other words not only paddy but also in the cases of all agricultural products, it is the peasants who are deprived by the middlemen. During the regime of any government, the domestic wants of the peasants have not been mitigated. Incidentally during all the regimes, the middlemen and agents are being considerably benefited.

It may be remembered here that sometime also due to the abnormal rise of the prices of vegetables, the Chief Minister Mamata Banerjee herself came down to the streets in visiting the market places in the Kolkata City. Following her laudable instance, other leaders and ministers in different districts also visited the market places in their respective areas for a few days. The administrative big shots also dispensed with their inertia of rest. But in reality the total situation remained unaltered. The middlemen are throwing dust in everybody's eyes and continuing their evil practices as usual. The administrative authorities are continuing to stick to their usual indifferent attitude or simply continuing to connive at the middlemen. The Chief Minister also along with the other members of the cabinets is being busy with other involvements. Nobody seems to have any time to concern himself with the problem of investagating how the middlemen are exploiting the poor and helpless peasants without any hindrance from any quarters.

The Food Minister Jyotipriya Mallik has observed : We simply lack an adequate infrastructure for directly purchasing paddy from the peasants. Therefore, we took help from the mill-owners. In other words, the government has knowingly left the fortune of the peasants in the hands of the middlemen.

Two questions may arise here. In the first place, what is the reason that the infrastructure for directly purchasing paddy from the peasants cannot be built up. Where actually is the shoe pinching? If in this matter the earlier government is a total failure, is then the new government taking new initiatives?

Secondly, even if we assume that for the time being there is no official infrastructure, why should not the present government have control and monitoring authority over the mill-owners.

Why should not the government gather adequate information about the way millowners are exploiting the hapless peasants in this way? And if such information does reach the government, why will it not immediately take adequate steps for remedying this miserable situation?

The government can ill afford to sit idle under such circumstances by putting the responsibility on anybody else's shoulder. The government will have to remember that instead of constituting ten or twenty committees with the members of the intelligentsia the priority in its programme of assistance is to maintain the interest of the peasants in travail. It will have to develop awareness about this priority. The previous government failed to understand this priority. If the present government also fails to appreciate this responsibility the citizens of the region will be utterly frustrated.

The Food Minister demands the new government has already spent Rs. 100 crores in purchasing paddy at support prices. But why Rs. 100 crores? The Food Minister can spend Rs. 500 crores on this account but if as a result of this public expenditure, the depressed peasant community is not benefited and on the contrary the middlemen and agents are the undesirable gainers, the real target of the government remains unfulfilled. In the present instance the target is really unfulfilled.

The last leftist government could not or rather did not remove this unholy dominance of the middlemen and agents. Rather these middlemen extended their hands even to the administrative machinery. No remarkable initiative to stop the mischievous activities of the middlemen is noticeable even now on the part of the new government.

All that has been done to stop these mischief-makers from their blood-sucking operations seems to be mere lip-service and there is no remarkable practical initiative. If like in the previous regime the middlemen again extend their dirty hands of interference in the administration of the new regime that will be an extremely unfortunate happening. Therefore by throwing a wet blanket on the evil designs of the blood-sucking middlemen, the new government will have to prove its sincerity in protecting the interests of the impoverished peasants.

44

OFFENDERS AT NANDIGRAM SHOULD BE SQUARELY PUNISHED

The criminal Investigation Department (CID) has in the month of October 2011 started inquiry about those hapless people who lost their habitats as a result of the joint operation of the CPI (M)' s cadres and the police during the land movement of Nandigram.

Very recently the CID officers visited and inspected different areas of Nandigram including Sonachura and enquired from the eyewitnesses about the day on which the carnage happened under the instructions of the previous Chief Minister-cum-Police Minister Buddhadev Bhattacharya.

Naturally the people of Nandigram are jubilant at this role of the CID after the change of government in the political scenario. The day of judgment which they were so long expecting has at last arrived at their door. This seems to be the impression of the aggrieved residents of Nandigram. Nothing new can be said about the infernal carnage committed at Nandigram in 2007 by the CPI(M) activists in alliance with the police. Not only mass massacre and massrape exactly, how many people were killed and kidnapped in that hullabalo are not accurately known even to this day. The relatives and family members of those missing persons are even now unaware what consequence ultimately befell in their fates.

The last left front government had made continuous efforts to cover up this nightmarish mass massacre from public attention. It was strange that this inhuman incident was elogised by the Regional secretary of CPI(M) Biman Basu who gave it a testimonial saying a 'new sunrise has taken place in Nandigram.' The residents of

Nandigram and various mass organisations have repeatedly been vocal in the demand of an impartial inquiry of this infernal incident. From different sources the demand for punitive measures has been raised against the culprits in Nandigram. But unfortunately even today the guilty persons involved in the tragic happenings of Nandigram have not been brought to book.

Not only West Bengal but the entire nation was embittered and enraged at the tragic massacre of Nandigram. Even outside the borders of India the Nandigram incident attracted the wrathful notice of umpteen millions. Distinguished persons with both national and international reputation condemned this incident in an indubious voice. But it is regrettable that the then leftist government were not ashamed at that matter. Rather they made an attempt to suppress the weeping residents of Nandigram under the boots of the police.

These oppressed people of Nandigram were so far waiting for receiving social justice. In the history of the land movement of the country, the incidents of Nandigram and Singur will be mentioned for ever with adequate importance. To speak the truth, the initiation of a political change in this region has started from the movements of singur and Nandigram. The sparks of protest was lit up in Singur and at Nandigram that spark was converted into a flame. It was that flame which in later days spread all over the region and burnt the CPI(M) regime to rack and ruin. It is by keeping that history of Nandigram and Singur moments in mind that the new government will have to pay respect and obeisance to the sentinels of these two movements. The new government has done the right thing by calling upon the CID in the inquiry about the missing persons of Nandigram.

During the regime of the left front government quite a few mass massacres took place with the joint villainy of police and the party cadres. Our hairs will stand on edge if we hear an account of these mass massacres at Marichjhampi, Chhota Angaria, Bijan Setu, Nandigram - the accounts of all these incidents are bloodcurdling. No proper inquiry was made in any of these carnages which happened during the left front government. Those who were responsible for or connected with the mass massacres were not punished in any manner. They moved about in open air with full security and are still now moving about in a fearless manner. Some of them are occupying high positions inside CPI(M). Some of them were posted in important official positions during the leftist government.

During the leftist regime the families of the victims who died in mass massacres went from door to door or from pillar to post but found no justice. Rather instead of justice, they were subjected to threatening by the party and the government. But to speak the truth those who were connected with these mass massacres were in a real sense enemies of civilization. They are averse to humanism. It is in the interest of humanism that they should be meted out adequate punishment.

Now the government has been altered. The new government has started once again a new inquiry by the CID in the Nandigram episode. We can only cherish the hope that that enquiry will result in giving proper punishment to the guilty persons involved in the Nandigram incident. At the same time we will also demand that fresh inquiries should be made into other episodes by the new government. This government should this time arrange for adequate punishment to all those persons who are remaining outside the clutches of law and order even after committing atrocious killing of innocent citizens.

45

FOCUS ON INNER CONFLICT

Almost six months have elapsed since the residents of West Bengal have received the taste of political change. This change has at last come at the conclusion of the nightmarish misrule of 34 years on the 8 crores of citizens of this region. The very clear popular mandate in this year's election was that -whatever be the means CPI(M) should be defeated. There was no clear idea regarding the exact shape of the change to be brought about. But what was certain was that the people earnestly yearned for freedom from the hands of CPI(M) which was dominanted by promoters, free footers armed cadres, fake industrialists and ill-reputed leaders like Lakshman Seth, Sushanta Ghosh, Anil Basu and Majid. Master etc. The ordinary citizens did not want to listen any further to the rodomontades of the day dreaming Chief Minister Buddhadev Bhattacharya who was at the helm of the hellish episodes of Nandigram and Netai. They did not wish to witness any further the gesticulations of Biman Basu or Goutam Dev. Such was the attitude prevalent among the common masses. That is why despite thousand macabre manipulations there appeared fissures on the red bastions of CPI(M) at Buddhadev Bhattacharya's Jadavpur, Goutam Dev's Dum Dum, Ashoke Bhattacharya's Siliguri, Asim Dasgupta's Khardaha, Nirupam Sen's Burdwan (south). Actually these infamous CPI(M) leaders became the eyesores of the ordinary citizens of West Bengal.

In the election of change the citizens have given their verdict against the evil practice of bossing against forcible collection of money, against the dominance of promoters, against the ruthless killing of the local residents in Jangalmahal, against the breakdown of law and discipline, against the joblessness of government offices, against the hospitals where medical services were unavailable, against restlessness and to cap it all, against a rotten and monotonous administrative system of 34 years. There was the universal expectation that only Mamata Banerjee is capable of appearing in the role of the saviour of the region from the misrule of CPI(M). It is the Trinamool Congress (TMC) which alone is an effective alternative to CPI(M) which for a long period appeared to have no viable alternative. That is why a change in the political scenario was urgently called for.

The much-yearned-for change actually arrived at last. But at the same time the Tsunami of change also appeared inside the new ruling party TMC as well and consequently the entire backbone of the party underwent a change. Those who were the earlier activists of TMC remained even now but they did not receive the taste of power. They are only bearing the happy memory of being the associates of Mamata Banerjee for a long period. They did not receive any official advantage. They are the majority in number. All these TMC activists really loved the party. Despite mental and physical persecution at the hands of CPI(M), they never thought of deserting the company of Mamata Banerjee. But after the party came to power in the region within these few months, most of them have lost their earlier authority. Inside the party they are the green TMC. On the other hand following the familiar rule of alteration of the government, the ruling party has now come to be dominated by the new entrants.

From the cabinet to administration in every branch of the party the new entrants have gained in influence and publicity. Most of them enjoyed the blessings of power during the CPI(M) regime to the fullest extent. Most of them have joined the TMC after the Lok Sabha election in 2009. The farsightedness of many such leaders or semi-leaders is admirable. About three years ago, they could very well preconceive that the days were altering. It will no longer pay to remain in CPI(M), rather it would be much more profitable to join TMC. In many cases lots of expenditure were incurred by many of them in the pursuit of winning the favours of many present leaders and ministers. Needless to say, by virtue of their own competence they have now been placed in suitable positions in the ruling party. Men who were earlier subordinate officers of CPI(M) have now become MLAs or ministers. Again a small trader who was a mastan in the favour of the earlier chief minister is now seen to accompany the present chief minister in her rural visits. The people of this category have been registered as

Red TMC inside the party. After the political change which came about in 2011 there is now a conflict between these two factions; Green TMC and Red TMC. To explain it further the conflict is between the old agencies and the presently discredited members of TMC and the new entrants and opportunists in TMC. The more their infighting inside the party will intensify the TMC after gaining the experience of winning numerous battles against CPI(M) will be faced with prospects of decline and downfall.

A few examples will clarify the issue of infighting *between* green TMC and red TMC to a greater extent.

Let us turn our attention to the Coochbehar district. In this district of North Bengal the fight between these two factions has assumed an acute shape. The leadership of the red TMC is in the hands of Hiten Barman who has become a minister in TMC after leaving *his* earlier party Forward Block. And the leadership of green TMC is in the hands of the old Trinamool leader Rabindranath Ghosh. Hitendra Babu has become the Forest Minister. He is entrusted with supervising everything from smuggled timber to seesaw mills. The opportunity of both enjoying and demonstrating power is plenty in this department. On the other hand Rabindranath Babu has received the charge of somehow operating the North Bengal Transport with subsidies. His days are busy with the task of making appeal for finance to the Transport Minister. At this opportunity the leaders who came recently from Forward block to TMC has taken over the charge of running the party in the district. At the present moment there is going on a skirmish between green TMC and Red TMC in different *blocks* of the Coochbehar district.

Let us now turn to Nanur. Rana Sinha, who was the terror of Nanur and the confidential assistant of five Forward Block Ministers is now in TMC. After the change in government, the district Chairman of TMC, Anubrata Mondal has given him the charge of running the party in the district. Witnessing this, those who have been fighting for long in Nanur are dismayed like anything. They are thinking that this is indeed a strange phenomenon. All their lives they have been fighting a bitter struggle against those who have now become their leaders after the transfer of power. This is a fact with which they cannot agree.

A direct confrontation has already started between the MLA of Nanur Gadadhar Hazra and the district chairman Anubrata Mandal (Keshta). It is learnt that in Birbhum everybody belonging to green TMC is now a supporter of the MLA of Nanur. However the leaders of the red TMC are also not ready to admit defeat. Because most of the important areas of the party have already been brought under their manipulation and domain. As a consequence of the conflict between red TMC and green TMC a half-leader has been sent to jail in Bardhaman's Mangalkote on charges of forcible multing of money. It is alleged that the police and administration are at the beck and call of the red TMC leaders. Consequently green TMC has now been confronted with acute danger. In case of the slightest disorder the green TMC leaders are being imprisoned. Thus, the situation is much like the condition prevailing during the earlier regime.

But there are also many opposite events. In North 24 Parganas right before the eyes of the national minister Mukul Roy the green TMC leader and activists have hit with a broomstick the local M.P, Nurul Islam. Mr. Islam is a votary of the red TMC.

His offence was that he took the strategy of taking into the party an illreputed person called Babu Master. The thrashing that was given to him of course made him alter his mind.

Again in Rajarhat-New Town the scenario are like this. The stalwarts of red TMC are building up different syndicates in the name of MA-MATI-MANUSH and indulging in forcible collection of money from different peoples in an unrestrained manner. Only yesterday these people were in the shelter of CPI(M). In Mandirbazar of South 24 Parganas the situation is far more critical. A few leaders and supporters of CPI(M) after committing murder have taken shelter in TMC in order to get protection from the clutches of law. The family of the murdered person (belonging to green TMC) is moving from post to pillar, but everywhere the red TMC people are so strong that the murderers who have recently altered their political career are safely moving about in the public for the 'offence' of being vocal against the misdeeds of the red TMC people. The green TMC leader Tapan Datta of Bally has been assassinated.

At Singur a red TMC legislator is up and doing in the matter of removing a green TMC minister. At Nandigram in order to protest against the whimsical activities of a red TMC leader the workers and officers of the East Medinipur Zilla parishad undertook a ceasework. The red TMC has spread its influence not only over the party but also over the branch organisations of TMC.

For example in the TMC organization of the doctors in Barasat there is one guilty ENT specialist who was only the other day a leader of the doctors' organisation of CPI(M). The woman leader of the Trinamool Trade Union is a red TMC. As a matter of fact from the Trinamool trade union the green TMCs have all been driven away by the red TMCs. Consequently wherever there is a labour union the mudsling between the green TMC and the red TMC is assuming an ugly shape.

Not only inside the party but also inside the government as well the division between the green TMC and red TMC is very much conspicous now. In the matter of running the government also the clout of red TMC is comparatively greater. Mamata has kept her old compatriots with befitting honour in the regional cabinet but she has failed to do adequate winnowing in reshuffling her bureaucracy. Involuntarily there has occurred a division between the Bengalees and the non-Bengalees among the IPS Officers.

It is true that during the left front regime CPI(M) did not attach much importance to the Bengalee IPS officers. But going to give importance to the Bengalees how could a gram panchayat Pradhan, Bardhaman of CPI(M) Madan Ghosh became the superintendent of Police in a district like Howrah. How does a person like Tanmoy Roy Choudhury even now manage to remain the Superintendent of Police in the Hooghly district with the notorious record of firing on innocent villagers in Nandigram. If only the jersey is changed, a heinous offence cannot certainly be washed away. If the new Chief Minister makes a little inquiry she will come to have the impression that those who are enjoying the support of the red TMC activists are giving indulgence to such guilty officers in the administration.

The Chief Minister Mamata Banerjee is of course aware of the unseemly contest between the green TMC and the red TMC inside the party. Greater knowledge about this matter can be expected from the two leaders Mukul Roy and Subrata Baxi. Because these two gentlemen even now regularly sit in the Trinamool Bhavan and give a patient hearing to the grievances of the party leaders. Perhaps in view of this terrible tendency Mamata has hastily called election in the party. The purpose is to bring the really capable persons in running the party to the forefront. At this critical moment the TMC leadership will have to remember that if the party somehow goes into the grip of the red TMC, the circumstances will go out of control.

Because about the red TMC people, CPI(M)'s opinion is that they were merely floodwater which earlier brought about a rot in their earlier organisation. It is a great relief that they have shifted their allegiance to TMC. These red TMC people who were the back bone of CPI(M) are now the epicentre of power inside the TMC. In case an earthquake breaks out the entire party will break down. Because the other contestant the green TMC, although they are more numerous, have not yet tasted power. Most of them belong to the grassroot level of TMC. Of course the leaders of the ruling party are certainly aware of all these matters. The matter to watch is whether they can take any remedial measures in the organisational election. Those ordinary citizens who have elected the party to victory want to see that at the forefront should remain leaders who are cultured, considerate, transparent, honest and capable to win the admiration of the common masses.

46

PRICE-RISE AND ALL THAT

The price-rise of food articles has exceeded 10% in the week which ended on October 8. The price-rise of food articles in the country has increased to the extent of 10.60%. Consequently the prices of food articles like spices, fruits, vegetables, milk, fish, meat, eggs etc. have increased by leaps and bounds. This information has been revealed by the national government.

At the same time from the statistics submitted by the national government in the week ended on the last August 20, the rise in prices of food articles exceeded the limit of 10% in a similar manner. From the statistics submitted by the national government it is known that in the annual account on the week ended on 8th October, the prices have increased most in the case of spices and vegetables. The amount of this price-rise is 17.59%. In one year vegetable prices have increased 18%. The prices of eggs, fish and meat have increased 14.10%. The prices of fruits have increased by 12.39 per cent. The price of milk has risen by 10.60%. The prices of pulses have risen by 7.42%. In this annual account it is seen that in the week ended on 8th October, it is seen that the price of rice has increased by 4.42%.

The crisis does not end here. It has been known that in response to this inflationary price-rise Reserve Bank may very soon raise the Repo rate of interest. Consequently it was apprehended that the real or reverse repo rates of interest of the commercial banks in the cases of cars and houses and personal credits may be hiked further.

In order to combat inflationary price-rise from the month of March 2010 uptil now, the RBI has increased its money rate or repo rate of interest at least twelve times. If the RBI once again raises this rate of interest, those middle class service holders who took loan from commercial banks for purchasing houses and cars will be in jeopardy. Taking all things together, it may be presumed that the circumstances are gradually becoming straitened,

When there was a crash in the American economy and consequently there was a worldwide great depression, many people opined that in the case of India owing to the farsightedness of Manmohan Singh that recession has been resisted at least to some extent. This assertion has some partial validity. The blast of worldwide recession hit India to some extent, but the Indian economy was not affected in the same manner as the economies of the western nations like the U.S.A. After resisting that blast of depression, India has now been affected by the current inflation. And whatever the public opinion about it, it is a fact that during the last one year all the efforts of the UPA government in resisting infl ation and price-rise have been virtually frustrated. During the last year the present government could not at all bring inflation under control.

In the case of India one of the causes of this infltionary price-rise is the parallel economy of black money. The RBI has repeatedly emphasised the recovery of this hidden volume of black money in the nation in combating inflation. UPA government also repeatedly issued the threatening of recovering the black money hidden in the national economy. Reference has also been made occasionally to the need for recovering the total volume of black money of the Indians accumulated in foreign countries.

But apart from enlivening the media and keeping it warm the national government failed to show any remarkable initiative in recovering the black money. The impact of the worldwide depression could not certainly be avoided by India and it will be definitely felt in this country sooner or later.

But if at the sametime the national government could take at least some active steps in recovering black money, if it could actually succeed in breaking down the parallel economy of black money price-rise could not be skyrocketing. Middle classes and lower classes could not have fallen in such great crises. But no initiatives of the national government in the matter of breaking *down* the black *economy* were noticed so far.

During the last one year the UPA government has failed in many instances. Among them the failures of the UPA government in existing inflation and price-rise are most glaring. No such possibility is visible in the near future that the national government could succeed in adopting any immediately effective step. Although the national Finance Minister Pranab Mukherjee expressed the hope that near about the month of March 2012 inflation may come down to the level of 7%.

Even if this expectation continues to be true the citizens of the nation will have to carry out the burden of inflation for the coming four months. Already Congress is bewildered by the critical problem of inflationary price-rise. The other partners of UPA like TMC and DMK are unwilling to share this responsibility with the major partner.

Another partner of UPA is NCP whose leader is the national Agriculture Minister Sharad Pawar who has declared in no uncertain terms that this is not one of his responsibilities. It is clear that he has blamed the Congress for the entire matter.

In case the UPA government under the leadership of Congress Party fails to imprison the evil spirit of inflationary price-rise in the bottle at an early period, no one can foretell with certainty their probable future in the coming election. No one can indicate with emphasis that in the ultimate analysis the current inflation will not turn out to be the principal reason of crackdown of UPA in the next election.

47

RESERVE BANK'S ADVICE TO REGIONAL GOVERNMENT

In the context of the current financial crisis of West Bengal the Governor of Reserve Bank, D. Subba Rao has recently given it some advices. A few days ago he has commented in Kolkata that there is only one way to come out of the crisis through which the region is currently passing, that is, the government will have to increase its own earnings and cut down its expenditures. About reducing its expenditure two matters should be taken into account. Essential expenditures should of course be incurred but at the same time alertness must be maintained so that inessential expenditures are brought down. Although the Governor of the Reserve Bank did not utter it explicitly the message that it has given to the regional government is that the government cannot be run by depending only on loans and grants. If the government is to be managed in a really efficient manner the illusions of cheap popularity should be dispelled and the positive thoughts of increasing the fiscal revenues should be concentrated upon. There is of course the possibility that this sort of advice from the RBI may not please many higher-ups of the regional government. But those who have strong sense of realism will admit that the Governor of RBI has actually prescribed a correct remedy. Previously the national Finance Minister Pranab Mukherjee also gave the same advice to the regional government.

The majority of the politicians in our country cannot succeed in winning freedom from the illusion of cheap popularity. They always suffer from the apprehension that in case firm steps are adopted with a view to ensuring economic reform, popularity in electoral politics will perhaps be at stake. From this apprehension derives the politics of making things available. This politics thereafter becomes a burden on the shoulders of the government as an inevitable consequence of which the government bows down. The greatest instance in this matter is West Bengal. During the last 34 years in pursuance of the politics of cheap popularity the left front government has drained off the public treasury of the region. They have bowed out from the political pulpit after imposing a huge burden of public debt on the shoulders of the regional government.

No doubt a new government has come to power. But they are puzzled to understand how this huge burden of public debt of the previous government will be squarely dealt with. The authorities of the new government are simply bewildered to find out the way of redemption of this huge public debt and carry on the developments activities of the government.

Without trying to find out means for increasing the fiscal finance the previous government was unwisely offered with the illusory pursuits of cheap popularity and left the public treasury into shambles from which the authorities of the new government could uptil now find no way out.

Nobody expects that from this miserable economic crisis the region can be recovered overnight. In actual reality, this matter is a time-consuming process. But in order to come out from this imbroglio the government will have to take initiatives from right now. It should take careful lessons from the ways suggested by the Governor of the RBI and reduce the inessential expenditures with increasing the fiscal revenues. The government will have to practise abstinence and carefully think out the ways in which revenues must be increased.

It is a matter for regret that the new government is also failing to win freedom from the illusion of cheap expensive popularity among the masses. Consequently just as there are blemishes in the list of priorities of the government, there is also a hike in the official expenditure in the unproductive account. The proof of this proposition has been obtained in the recent hike of the allowances of the ministers and legislators and the official decision to give 10% dearness allowance to the government employees. It was the Chief Minister Mamata Banerjee who herself commented previously that within Rs. 1.00,96 paise are spent for repaying the debts and giving salaries to the government employees. Nonetheless it was she again who herself increased the expenditure on this account at this period of acute financial crisis. As a result of this declaration additional 3 thousand crores of rupees will be annually spent from the public treasury and not unlike the previous government, the new government will also feel called upon to raise finance from the market by issuing bonds. Just as in the past, the left front government advanced in the path of paying salaries by borrowing finance from the market the new government is also actually following the same precedent.

If the government is really determined to enhance the fiscal finance, it is necessary to impose taxes in certain spheres. But the Chief Minister of the region and TMC leader Mamata Banerjee is not in this case willing to move away from the path of popularity although new government has not yet found any alternative avenue for enhancing incomes.

The Governor of RBI has commented that it is easy to talk about enhancing income by cutting down inessential expenditures. But this is actually a hard nut to crack. And if West Bengal is determined to come out of this shell of financial crisis, it is urgently necessary to perform that difficult task. This is really a monstrous challenge before the Chief Minister of the new government.

48

PLIGHT OF RURAL HOSPITALS

An extensive crisis of oxygen has appeared in the government hospitals of the rural areas of Hooghli and South 24 Parganas. In different blocks like Hooghli's Khanakool Haripal and Dhaniakhali, the rural hospitals of the highest lands have either 2 or 1 oxygen cylinders in their hands. From the official statistics it is known that in the rural hospitals of the block levels in Hooghly and South 24 Parganas the stocks of oxygen cylinders are like this: Khanakool 2, Dhaniakhali-2; in Raidighi only 4 among the 34 cylinders are full, in Sagar almost all the 19 cylinders are empty; in Mandir Bazar there are only 2 cylinders. But in the Khanakool rural hospital of Hooghli there is the responsibility of the treatment of 2 lakhs 43 thousands of people of that Block, in the Dhaniakhali rural hospital rests the responsibility of treatment of 3.5 lakh people. In the Purshura Block Primary Health Centre rests the charge of treatment of 1 lakh 73 thousand local residents. The physicians there are compelled to bring oxygen cylinders from outside.

Under the circumstances the two block medical officers raised an important question. They have made the comment that in the winter numerous patients will require oxygen. But we are not getting oxygen. If therefore there is any scandal in the hospital for not providing oxygen, will the responsibility for that devolve on us? These doctors have spoken out absolute truth. If due to the want of necessary medical treatment, the local residents raise protest in those hospitals, who will bear the responsibility? The local residents or the physicians of the hospital or the regional Health Department ?

It has been known that this crisis of oxygen started even before the Pujas. Presently it has assumed a more acute shape. In other words in these district hospitals despite the fact that oxygen cylinders were unavailable in these hospitals from before the Pujas the Health authorities remained inactive. It is clear now that so long they remained silent and took no necessary steps. The Special Secretary of the Health Department Sanjoy Mitra has observed : 'I have heard the matter. The direction to adopt the necessary measures has been issued.' Needless to say that he has talked in the familiar method of the bureaucrats. Oxygen cylinders are unavailable in the rural hospitals. But the Special Secretary of the Health Department is completely silent about the reason why attempts to solve the crisis were not made, or when the necessary measures will be adopted? This attitude of the Health authorities give the impression that the rural hospitals and health centres have only secondary importance. It is not necessary to pay much attention towards this direction.

There can be no hesitation in commenting that the rural hospitals and health centres have all along received the neglect and disaffection of the health authorities. After the new government came to power, the Chief Minister Mamata Banerjee has made many sudden visits to the government hospitals of Kolkata. Consequently the standard of services in those hospitals has improved to some extent. But the rural hospitals and health centres escaped the notices of everybody. They are staying in the same darkness in which they had been remaining earlier.

Even now rural hospitals mean places without adequate infrastructures where cattle move about without any restriction and where visits for adequate medical treatment are almost always infructuous since there is lack of adequate infrastructures. Many doctors are unwilling to be posted in rural hospitals and health centres. The left front government did not take initiatives to improve their state of management notwithstanding their continuance in power for 34 years. Yet if adequate infrastructure could be provided their standards of services could have been much improved and the extra pressure on the urban hospitals could have been much relieved.

It is principally the indigent families of lower class who come for medical treatment to these rural hospitals. They do not have the finance to come for medical treatment to the cities. But they have also

replied : I cannot give any such guarantee. If the barrel-wise price goes up in the international market, the domestic price of petrol will of course be hiked.

The TMC MPs asked the Prime Minister : But where will this process be concluded? A meeting has already been called on 26 November over the hike in the prices of cooking gas, diesel and kerosene. Apprehension will be expressed there about further hikes in prices.

The Trinamool MPs expressed anxiety and opined that in this way pressure is being continuously mounted on the ordinary citizens. The Prime Minister disregarded this anxious question and looked straight at the face of the Railways Minister Dinesh Trivedi and commented in a cold voice. 'You are a member of the Cabinet. It has not been proper on your part to disclose in this way the secret message of the cabinet.' In great uneasiness Dinesh Tribedi shook his head and tried to protest that he did not disclose any official secret. But before he could speak anything Kalyan Banerjee intervened and said: He did not tell anything. It is actually the Petroleum Minister, Jaipal Reddy who gave this information to the media. In fact we have come to know this information from the newspaper titled Economic Times. This time the Prime Minister on his part fell in great uneasiness and murmured, God alone knows what is the rule truth. At least I did not have any such information in advance!

The Prime Minister remained silent for sometime and then commented : Much capital has to be invested in the social sector. Different social projects are going on. I am asking you to comment yourself how this can be possible if fiscal finances are not increased. No, no. There cannot be any argument about lowering the price of petrol. Trinamool MPs raised the question : Then you should suggest some other way of bringing down the price of petrol. Manmohan singh shook his head and replied : It is better if you yourselves could advise the regional government to cut somewhat the fixed expenditure. This will definitely result in much benefits!

Sudip Banerjee et al argued that we are the second largest partner in the UPA-2 alliance. But none of its decisions is available to us. This is not good for the politics of alliance. The Prime Minister seemed to concur somewhat with this grievance and said : Yes, in future days we should of course pay attention to adequate discussion with all the partners. But it appears to me that the coordination committee about which you are so anxious is unnecessary. Everybody remains present in the Cabinet meetings. That is why.....".

It is obvious that the UPA-2 government has suddenly taken a strict position regarding its principal partner. The TMC MPs have also admitted that so much stiff attitude was never before noticed in the case of Manmohan Singh. They were all really perplexed. Very naturally Mamata Banerjee after hearing this information from Mukul Roy was highly enraged. Because just when the Prime Minister was taking this stiff attitude to the TMC MPs in New Delhi at that time in Kolkata the national Finance Minister Pranab Mukherjee and Mamata Banerjee met in a conference. And in that conference also Mukherjee did not give any hopeful information to Mamata Banerjee. Far from giving any assurance of providing finance according to need Mukherjee gave her the unpalatable advice to procure their own finance by their own efforts. He has opined in unmistakable terms that there has occurred no reason for providing a greater quantum of finance to West Bengal in comparison to other regions precisely because in the perspective of the federal structure this happening is impossible.

The question that is uppermost in the minds of everybody is what might be the possible reason for the indifence of the UPA government about its principal partner. A lot of theories have emerged at the time of analysing this strange attitude.

Congress has already been marginalised by instances of corruption and scandals and consequently it is not desirous to drag the present government till 2014. It is planned that the election should be held much earlier. That is why if TMC withdraws its support and consequently the national government collapses, Congress just does not care. Rather amidst a thousand infamies the status of a martyr party will provide some additional advantage.

The protagonists of this theory believe that the level of mercury in the barometer of ambition regarding Rahul Gandhi inside the national government and the Congress Party has come down to a great extent. In other words the confidence with which it was presumed that he will come and conquer in the arena of politics was actually not noticed. Even now so far as political wisdom and clout are concerned, Rahul Gandhi is still now remaining in the average scoring ground. The probability that in the scheduled election of 2014 the popularity of Congress Party i.e. the UPA government will suddenly be skyrocketing is still now not noticeable. Rather there are indications that in the coming days more scandals will come to light.

Indications are also available that many other big shots are involved in the 2G Spectrum incident of corruption. That is why if the UPA government does break down and thereafter the Congress Alliance fails to come to power then for a pretty long time Rahul Gandhi will receive the advantages of becoming the opponent party leader. It is much more acceptable to gain popularity by becoming leader of the opposition party than to become a flop by making efforts to come to power as the leader of the government. Because no matter which government comes to power, this inflationary trend and the price-rise of petrol will not be easily resisted. Thousand other issues will accompany this incident. In this way by staying out of government for a few years the government will accumulate strength and power. It is certain that during that period there will be some 'Khichri' government in the centre. That government will of course not be able to continue for five years. Therefore after its fall Congress will return to power in its own glory. That strong government will be piloted in a capable manner by Rahul Gandhi himself.

Another view point is that all this is nothing. It is presumed that even if TMC withdraws its support the national government will not collapse. Mulayam Singh Yadav, Mayabati and even the leftists will of their own accord come forward to save it from breaking down. Because if an election in case of a possible breakdown of the national government is held none of the presently existing parties has the necessary strength to face that election. None of them is actually certain about its real strength. There are also misgivings about the fact whether even the foremost opponent party BJP at all wants interim election, because a regionwise analysis will reveal that just as Congress will perform miserably in many regions and fail to reach the figure 207. Similarly notwithstanding good performance in some regions BJP will face disaster in many other regions. Among the *second group* Karnataka is one. Apart from that BJP also lacks adequate partners for its alliance. Only the Sanjukta Janata Dal of Nitish Kumar is capable of winning 20 to 30 seats. It can be foretold right now that in the next election Shiromoni Akali Dal will cut a sorry figure and even if the number of MPS of Shiv Sena remains more or less the same, what will be its impact on the total situation. On the other hand if the NDA attempts to form the government at the centre by way of increasing the strength of its alliance, *will* that attempt be appreciated by the leftists or Mulayam Singh Yadav or Mayabati? Therefore notwithstanding the existence of a thousand *crises* Congress has presupposed that the government at the national level is not *going* to fall. That is why the programme has been taken to poohpooh for the time being the harangues of TMC.

The question that may be raised now is regional, Congress has made alliance with TMC at both the national and levels. Can *anybody* in that party from the topmost leadership to the grassroot level - workers sincerely desire that the West Bengal government under the leadership of Mamata Banerjee should be considered as a totally successful regional government? The Congress party which has been reduced to a signboard and the anti-left support has been monopolised by Mamata Banerjee from the headquarters at her Kalighat residence can certainly ill afford to forget that humiliation. Uptil now neither Ajoy Mukherjee nor Pranab Mukherjee nor Priyaranjan Dasmunshi could turn it into an insignificant entity after coming out of its predominant position. But Mamata has succeeded in this feat by her lone efforts. It is difficult for Congress to forget that humiliation and anger. Therefore it can be certainly foretold that the national Congress government will never take a liberal attitude to render all kinds of help to her in order to assist her government to ascend to the vertex of success. Rather the opposite attitude is likely in the Indian politics. In other words, in order to recover its own lost glory by slow or quick means Congress will have no stones unturned in causing obstacles to Mamata Banerjee's government at each and every step. There can be little doubt that the more faux pas will be taken by this government the more elated Congress will become not unlike the leftists.

And this fact is not unknown to Mamata Banerjee and she is also not unaware that this mischievous design is engineered by Sonia Gandhi herself.

It is quite likely that she has already realised that the national government in New Delhi with a view to discrediting her regional government *will* indirectly use the weapon of economic deprivation in this manner. When no additional help can be expected this sham friendship of UPA government through outward support is simply meaningless.

Therefore Mamata also has taken the decision that she should loterate this far and no farther and get prepared for witnessing the coming contest in panchayat election: CPI(M) versus TMC versus Congress. In comparison to the earlier elections it will become a much more interesting chapter in West Bengal's regional parties: 10 Janpath Road vs 30B Harish Chatterjee Street.

50

WEST BENGAL, BANGLADESH AND THE TISTA TREATY

West Bengal will cooperate with Bangladesh as much as possible regarding the distribution of water of the Tista river. In the month of November the Chief Minister Mamata Banerjee has given this assurance to the Foreign Minister of Bangladesh, Dipu Mani. In a conference with the Foreign Minister Mamata has said that in the matter of distribution of water of the Tista, West Bengal will render all kinds of assistance to Bangladesh. But which Bengal will receive how much water will he determined not at the political level but by the experts. The Chief Minister has informed that recently a Commission has been formed by keeping the river specialist Kalyan Rudra in mind. After this discussion with the Chief Minister, the two countries have come to believe that they will be enabled to proceed along a positive path about the Tista treaty.

In the month of September during the visit of Prime Minister Manmohan Singh to Bangladesh, the Tista Treaty was scheduled to be drawn up. But at the last moment Mamata Banerjee raised objection about the treaty and refused to accompany the Prime Minister in his visit to Bangladesh. Ultimately the treaty was not signed in the absence of Mamata Banerjee. The government of Bangladesh also was aggrieved at this fact of not signing this treaty. The heads of the two governments could perceive that unless Mamata Banerjee was appeased the future of that treaty was totally dark. From that period the government of Bangladesh had been trying to arrange a confidential meeting of Mamata Banerjee with the Prime Minister of Bangladesh Sheikh Hasina.

Bangladesh believes that such a meeting will to a great extent help in unfastening the gordian knot. To speak the truth, with this purpose in view the Foreign Minister of Bangladesh after attending a programme at Bengaluru rushed to Kolkata. Dipu Mani's objective was that a bridge should be built up for arranging a meeting between Sheikh Hasina and Mamata Banerjee. From that point of view this visit of the Foreign Minister of Bangladesh is quite successful. Because a few days later Prime Minister Sheikh Hasina will visit Kolkata. It is then that the Hasina-Mamata meeting will take place.

Altogether 54 rivers are flowing through India and Bangladesh among which there are the Ganga, the Tista, the Feni, the Ichhamati etc. Previously there was a long conflict between India and the erstwhile East Pakistan over the treaty regarding the distribution of water of the Ganga river. After the then Chief Minister of West Bengal entered into a treaty of distribution of water in 1996 that dispute came to be solved. But over the distribution of the Tista and the Feni, India still now has difference of opinion with Bangladesh. As the fall out of the Tista treaty, India will have to give more water to Bangladesh but it will become the gainer as the consequence of the Feni treaty. As the Tista treaty was not signed during the Dacca visit of India's Prime Minister as a protest, Bangladesh refused to sign the Feni treaty.

Consequently the future prospects of both the treaties are uncertain. It is true that around the Tista treaty not only West Bengal, Sikkim has also some objections. In case the Tista treaty is drawn up, it is alleged that there will be a crisis of irrigation water in the hilly areas including north Bengal. Similarly again Tripura will gain much in case of the Feni treaty.

Chief Minister Mamata Banerjee has asserted that the quantum of water to be received by a country will not be decided at the political level. On the contrary it will be settled by the experts. In this respect she has uttered the exactly right words. Till now no bipartite settlement has been arrived at regarding the distribution of water of the Tista. Both Bangladesh and India have respectively advanced their own view points, as a result of there being no joint survey, the controversy over the distribution of waters of the Tista continues to persist even to this day. That is why the proposal advanced by the Chief Minister is acceptable even now. But the expert committee that has to be constituted in this respect should ideally accommodate the impartial persons of both the countries.

At the same time at the time of drawing up the treaties regarding the Tista or the Feni, the Heads of the governments of both India and Bangladesh should remember the relevant lessons of history in the sub-continent between India and Bangladesh. The length of this frontier is 2 thousand 979 kilometers. Right from the time of the independence India had conflict with East Pakistan over this frontier. Even after the birth of Bangladesh that conflict has not been resolved as yet.

In 1975 the then Head of the state Sheikh Mujibar Rehman wanted to solve the border conflict by an agreement. Those who have conducted researches on the assassination of Mujib assert that Pakistan and its friend China did not want that this treaty should be materialised. That is why Mujib was assassinated with the help of the Pakistani agents. Both India and Bangladesh should remember that Pakistan and China do not want that a friendly relation should grow up between them. If the India-Bangladesh disagreement over the Tista and Feni continues there will be reason for elation of both Pakistan and China. Without allowing them the scope for elation if both Bangladesh and India sacrifice somewhat their respective interests and come to a common understanding, both of them will be benefited in the long run to a great extent.

51

PROBLEMS OF TOURISM IN NORTH BENGAL

Those who usually denounce the authorities are condemning the new Tourism Minister for the reason that uptil now he could not manage to pay a visit to North Bengal. Already many ministers of small, medium and big statures had occasions to pay visit to this area. Some of them came here more than once, some accompanied the Chief Minister, some of them came in connexion with the business of their own departments, some visited for their personal purposes or by virtue of some relations. But the Tourism Minister happens to be the only exception.

But we are all aware that both in the national and international arenas tourism in West Bengal means the hills and forests of this region. But without a separate department for north Bengal or the special thoughts of the new Chief Minister has lightened the responsibility or importance of the new minister can only be friendly the critics who are in the habit of denouncing the government. Those who are the traders of tourism can also explain whether the expansion of tourism can very well proceed without even the personal presence of the Tourism Minister. But those who have even very slight connection with this service can assert that the little development which has taken place in the sphere of tourism in north Bengal so far was never very extensive. Not only that its spread and intensity till today have been so little that they failed to serve the purpose of tourism of ordinary citizens.

Those people who are seen everyday to travel in congested buses inside the city or trains in the downtown areas under pressure of heavy crowds whenever they get the occasion rush to the side of hills, fountains or tea gardens or to the gates of the forest conservatories. Uptil now no government of either colour concerned themselves with their unshackled madness or limited financial capabilities.

Let us think of the experience of the people fifteen years earlier. When the tourism service has reached the international level in Rajasthan, Kerala or Madhya Pradesh, in West Bengal the tourist lodges meant ramshackle bedsteads, the nuisance of rats running helter skelter, windows with broken glasses and prehistoric airconditioning machines etc.

Thereafter a change was noticed in the situation. Reforms and changes in the circumstances of the tourist lodges began to appear. Popularity started increasing but at the same time service charges also went on being hiked, so much so that very soon these charges went outside the capacities of the Bengalee tourists with poor monthly incomes. How much per cent of the total number of tourists can bear the expenses of food and lodging with the entire family for two nights in Jaldapara tourist lodge today ? In the restaurant of Kurseong Tourist Lodge on the road to Darjeeling if a team of eight to ten persons enter for lunch or breakfast, their per capital expenses can never be cut below Rs. 100/. But 75% of the tourists who come to visit the hilly areas of Dooars have a daily per capital budget of not more than Rs. 750/. Hence the idea is gradually being deeprooted in the public psyche that government visits are invariably highly costly. The lodges of the Forest Development Corporation are comparatively less costly but their number also is limited. Profits from these circumstances are being made by non-governmental package tour at whose hands are victimised the low-budget tourists.

Not only the ordinary tourists but also those who derive their income from employment in tourism also should be considered in this context. Today all of us are more or less aware that the new name of tourism now is 'eco-tourism' which includes tourists, environment and the local aboriginals, and everybody's interest is preserved. But once a distinguished leader raised the question that 'It is very well understood that 'eco-tourism' means 'ecological' or 'ecofriendly' but can it at all be 'economical'? It is strange that in this question is hidden its positive answer. As a result of the initiatives of the divisional forest department of north Bengal thoughts of eco-tourism have been implemented in reality. But here also the development of the tribals of the forest has been taken into account and the ordinary tourists have been neglected. The Ghatakpur eco-camp of Sinchal Forest Conservancy or Ramsai Chino camp of Gorumara National Garden are in a word, unique but these are outside the capabilities of the lovers of tourism afflicted with wanderlust.

Very naturally, here arises the question of 'community tourism'. Ethically in this rural tourism based on communities both pleasure and profits can be derived by both the ordinary tourists as well as the ordinary local indigent people. But what has been noticed so far in the name of 'community tourism' although there are a few isolated attempts are actually a 'kind of exploitation'- the "cunning efforts" of a few urban traders under the garb of 'welfare', year after year have passed. In any of the villages of north Bengal, no remarkable socio-economic development came to the notice of anybody through the medium of community development. Because there was not the slightest effort or good will for participation or intervention or policy determination.

Under the circumstances we can raise a very easy question. The only region in India is West Bengal where the coexistence of the Himalaya sea-mangrove is not the only word, this is the only region in the country which can be self-reliant in the matter of its own tourist potential. Why then is it difficult to make tourism a populist programme here. Let the question of the mountains forests and ocean remain apart, but tourism can be made popular by an easy medium - the holy places. In the north Bengal there are very ancient Shivaratri festival of Jalpesh or Baneshwar or the Srabani Purnima fair or the Rasmela of Madanmohan Bari of Coochbehar on which occasion there take place unimaginable congregrations of people. But it is strange that the tourism Department has not yet assumed any significant role.

Similarly the flow of tourists can easily be catalysed by the schools or colleges receiving government grants, with official directions. Summer camps and nature observation can be made compulsory in the syllabus. Can there be misgivings or scepticism in anybody's mind that this will lead to the spiritual development of the future generation as well as enlargement of the total volume of tourism throughout the length and breadth of north Bengal.

Farming is not possible in the sprawling areas of the Dooars due to the disturbances caused by the elephants. Is it a very difficult task to please the low-budget tourists with arrangements for earning alternative incomes at the panchayat level by erecting cottages with bamboos, straws and tins, or building up cooperatives of the local jobless young men and women and cultivating vegetables in the gardens, fishes in the tanks, hatching the eggs of ducks or raising the poultry of the gardens?

After the new government came to power the unrest in the hills has disappeared. The wind of peace and tranquillity has started blowing throughout north Bengal. After a long time has returned an ideal climate for development of tourism. The voice of a populist development of tourism has been heard in the new decision of North Bengal Regional Transport corporation. Every morning matching time with the trains arriving from Kolkata one after another buses are starting from New Jalpaiguri station for Darjeeling, Kalimpong and Gangtok. In the evening they are returning in order that the train for Darjeeling can be caught. Similarly at Malbazar tourist transport hub is being constructed very soon. Other buses going to the Dooars and various ends of the mountain will be ready, in other words the expenses of ordinary people to visit Dooars and the mountains will be cut down. The higher is the number of buses and the more regular they become, both the aspects of reliance and economy will be ensured.

But what thereafter? In the tourism map of the world the presence of this region resembles a fossil. Bringing about its development calls for much time and patience. Before that are needed some populist activities. For example tourism will not increase if only tents are fixed at the Baxa Fort, for reading there will be needed a hanging bridge on which people will walk on feet, repair of broken roadways upto the Sadar or chief town and light and sound show at the fort compounds. Citizens aged 60 or 70 will be enabled to visit the place at least for once in their life to recount the memories of the freedom struggle and the new generation will receive the opportunity to inquire about its roots of ancestry.

And the responsibility for its preservation will be entrusted on the local residents. They will eagerly guard their noble possessions. If tents are fixed only red scorpions and indigenous dogs will abound there. Profits will only be appropriated by tent contractors and consultants, who succeeded in earning lots of finance in the early regime and after changing their colours are now moving around the ministers of the new government. Much caution will be required to get relief from the evil influences of these selfseekers.

On the contrary we must find out and get in touch with those persons who are ignoring the light of publicity in the remote corners of forests and mountains in a painstaking effort to explain to the poor and indigent local residents the matter of community tourism, the acute necessity of giving up the terrilbly harmful addiction to wines and narcotics, the need for sports and a developed way of life.

52

ANATOMY OF KOLKATA MUNICIPAL CORPORATION

In order to resist any kind of construction in the city along with hospitals the Kolkata Municipal Act of 1980 is sufficient. This has been admitted by the senior officers of the KMC themselves. They are saying that in the civic legislation it is the KMC which has been invested with full powers to resist illegal constructions. Apart from that there is the Municipal Buildings Rule. It is mandatory to abide by the Municipal Buildings Rule in the field of constructing houses in the Kolkata civic area and this rule has been erected on the basis of the National Building Code. Consequently without enacting a new rule, the corporation can break down any illegal construction by virtue of the correct regulations.

Just a glance at the civic law can give one the idea regarding what sort of strict measures can be adopted by the Municipal Corporation on receipt of an allegation of illegal construction. In sections 400(1) and 400(8) of the Municipal Act, it has been clearly mentioned that if an inquiry reveals that there is an apprehension of a major danger or that there is a violation of the law the Corporation can decide to adopt suitable measures. In this case it can without giving the owner of the house any opportunity for hearing, demolish the building. In case of necessity it can also issue instruction to break down only the illegal portion of a house. If this law is examined in depth, it can never be asserted that the Corporation has been given no power to resist illegal construction. Rather it should be understood that by virtue of the power which rests in the hands of the Corporation it can pull down at any time any kinds of illegal construction.

The matter to regret is that although there is so much legal power in the hands of KMC, illegal construction is not being stopped. Nor is the KMC taking adequate measures to break down illegal constructions. Moreover taking advantage of the inactivity of the KMC illegal constructions are going on in full speed.

Even in the earlier days after big fire accidents in the city the indifference and dereliction on the part of the KMC came to the notice of the citizens. Such incidents are coming to our notice ever after the fire accident of the AMRI hospital. The KMC cannot deny the responsibility for such fire accidents. Now the question that may be raised here is, why notwithstanding the existence of sufficient law in its hands KMC is not taking adequate initiatives to resist illegal construction.

The lawyers of the Kolkata Municipal Building Tribunal are saying that the indifferent attitudes of the officers of the Building Department are the principal hindrances in the matter of pulling down the illegal constructions. The files relating to many illegal buildings have been deliberately destroyed. Behind this activity is operating a vicious circle. Although files are being asked for by the Tribunal, the officers of the Building Department are dilly-dallying in this matter. Quite a few officers of CMC are also saying that there is indifference in the matter of implementing the laws.

It is quite clear that due to the tendency of indulging in dereliction on the part of a section of workers and officers of KMC initiatives are not conspicuous in the matter of checking illegal constructions. When Subrata Mukherjee was the Mayor of Kolkata, he succeeded to a great extent in restoring the work culture of KMC. The opportunist circle in the KMC was brought under control at that time.

After Subrata Mukherjee bowed out from KMC, it has returned to its earlier practice of dereliction and inactivity. At the sametime the present Mayor of CMC Shobhan Chatterjee in an attempt to cover up this failure of the CMC has advanced a ridiculous argument. He has said that in many cases illegal constructions cannot be pulled down for reasons of human interest. The question that may be raised here is why cannot illegal constructions be prevented before these are actually started.

According to the civil laws before the construction of any building the blueprint of the building has to be sent to the Municipal Building Committee. It is only when their approval is received the Building Department gives the necessary permission for construction. If despite all these safeguards illegal constructions are erected. we can safely conclude that there are blemishes at the very beginning where some dishonest circle is active.

That apart, despite the existence of much power in the hands of KMC for resisting illegal constructions, the perpetrators of such constructions are escaping from the clutching of the law due to a ludicrous directive of the civic authorities. In this directive it has been observed that these portions of the construction which fall outside the main blueprint can be made legal by paying fines to the KMC. By virtue of this instruction many people are being enthused for legalising their illegal constructions after these are actually erected. Hospitals like AMRI wanted to avail themselves of this opportunity. And the KMC gave them the necessary permission without first enquiring whether the security arrangements of that illegal portions were proper or improper.

After the fire accident of the AMRI hospital, both the Mayor and the regional government should become alert. The work culture in the KMC must be brought back and that ludicrous directive must be cancelled so that arrangements may be made to grant sanction to the blueprints of houses in consonance with the prevalent law in this respect.

POSITIONS HELD BY MAMATA BANERJEE

01.01.1970 : General-Secretary, Mahila Congress (I), West Bengal, (P.M. Indira Gandhi, President-Sarvepalli Radhakrishnan). Bengal Chief Minister 1.1.1970. Ajoy Kumar Mukherjee Bangla Congress in United Front, Governor - Shanti Swaroop Dhavan.

01.01.1978 : Secretary, District Congress Committee (Indira) [D.C.C. (I)], Calcutta South (P.M. Morarji Desai, President Basappa Danappa Jatti (Acting) Bengal Chief Minister 01.01.1978 Jyoti Basu Communist Party of India (Marxist) in Left Front, Governor - Anthony Lancelot Dias.

01.01.1984 : Elected to 8th Lok Sabha (P.M. Indira Gandhi, President - Neelam Sanjiva Reddy).

General-Secretary, All India Youth Congress (I). (P.M. Indira Gandhi, President - Neelam Sanjiva Reddy).

01.01.1985 : Member, Committee on the Welfare of Scheduled Castes And Scheduled Tribes (P.M. Rajiv Gandhi, President -Zail Singh).

01.01.1987 : Member, National Council, All India Youth Congress (I) (P.M. Rajiv Gandhi, President - Zail Singh).

01.02.1987 : Member, Consultative Committee, Ministry of Home Affairs (P.M. Rajiv Gandhi, President - Zail Singh).

01.03.1987 : Member, Consultative Committee, Ministry of Human Resource Development (P.M. Rajiv Gandhi, President -Zail Singh).

01.01.1989 : Member, Executive Committee, Congress Parliamentary Party [C.P.P. (I)] (P.M. Rajiv Gandhi, President - Zail Singh).

01.01.1990 : Member, Executive Committee, Pradesh Congress Committee [P.C.C. (I)], West Bengal (P.M. Rajiv Gandhi, President - Zail Singh).

01.01.1991 : President, Youth Congress, West Bengal (P.M. Vishwanath Pratap Singh, President - Ramaswamy Venkataraman).

01.01.1991 : Re-elected To 10th Lok Sabha (2nd Term) (P.M. Chandrashekar, President - Ramaswamy Venkataraman).

Union Minister of State, Human Resource Development, Department of Youth Affairs and Sports; and Women and Child Development (P.M. Chandrashekar, President - Ramaswamy Venkataraman).

01.01.1993: Member, Committee on Home Affairs (P.M. Pamulapartienkata Narasimha Rao, President -Ramaswamy Venkataraman).

01.01.1996 : Member, Consultative Committee, Ministry of Home Affairs (P.M. Pamulaparti Venkata Narasimha Rao, President-Ramaswamy Venkataraman).

01.01.1996 : Member, Committee on Public Accounts (P.M. Pamulaparti Venkata Narasimha Rao, President- Ramaswamy Venkataraman).

01.02.1996 : Re-elected to 11th Lok Sabha (3rd Term) (P.m. 1/2/1996 Pamulaparti Venkata Narasimha Rao, President-Ramaswamy Venkataraman).

01.03.1996 : Member, Committee on Home Affairs (P.M. Pamulaparti Venkata Narasimha Rao, President- Ramaswamy Venkataraman).

01.04.1996 : Member, Consultative Committee, Ministry of Home Affairs (P.M. Pamulaparti Venkata Narasimha Rao, President-Ramaswamy Venkataraman).

Founded All India Trinamool Congress, and elected Chairperson,

All India Trinamool Congress. (Haradanahalli Dodde Gowda Deve Gowda, President - Shankar Dayal Sharma).

1/1/1998 : Re-elected to 12th Lok Sabha (4th term) (P.M. Inder Kumar Gujral, President - Shankar Dayal Sharma).

1/2/1998 : Chairman, Committee on Railways (P.M. Inder Kumar Gujral, President - Shankar Dayal Sharma).

01.03.1998 Member, General Purposes Committee (P.M. Inder Kumar Gujral, President - Shankar Dayal Sharma).

01.04.1998 : Member, Consultative Committee, Ministry of Home Affairs (P.M. Atal Bihari Vajpayee, President - K.R. Narayanan).

1/1/1999 : Re-elected To 13th Lok Sabha (5th Term) (P.M. Atal Bihari Vajpayee, President - K.R. Narayanan).

1/2/1999 : Leader, All India Trinamool Congress Parliamentary Party Lok Sabha (P.M. Atal Bihari Vajpayee, President - K.R. Narayanan).

1/3/1999 : Member, General Purpose Committee (P.M. Atal Bihari Vajpayee, President - K.R. Narayanan) 01.04.1999

Union Cabinet Minister, Railways (P.M. Atal Bihari Vajpayee, President - K.R. Narayanan) 01.01.2002 Member, Consultative Committee, Ministry of IndustrIes (P.M. Atal Bihari Vajpayee, President - K.R. Narayanan).

01.01.2003 : Union Cabinet Minister (without any portfolio) (P.m. Atal Bihari Vajpayee, President - K.R. Narayanan).

1/9/2004 : Union Cabinet Minister, Coal and Mines (P.M. Atal Bihari Vajpayee, President - K.R. Narayanan).

5/14/2004 : Re-elected to 14th Lok Sabha (6th term) (P.M. Atal Bihari Vajpayee, President - K.R. Narayanan).

05.15.2004 : Member, Committee on Personnel, Public Grievances, Law and Justice (P.M. Atal Bihari Vajpayee, President - K.R. Narayanan).

1/1/2006 : Member, Committee on Home Affairs (P.M. Manmohan Singh, President, Abdul Kalam).

06.06.2006 : Member, Committee on Home Affairs (P.M. Manmohan Singh, President Abdul Kalam).

1/1/2009 : Re-elected to 15th Lok Sabha (7th term) (P.M. Manmohan Singh, President Abdul Kalam).

2/1 /2009 : Union Cabinet Minister, Railways (P.M. Manmohan Singh, President Abdul Kalam).

03.01.2009 : Leader, All India Trinamool Congress Parliamentary Party, Lok Sabha (P.M. Manmohan Singh, President Abdul Kalam).

20/5/2011 The First Woman Chief Minister of West Bengal after a Landslide Victory of Trinamool Congress over the Left Front (P.M. Manmohan Singh, President Pratibha Patil).

Social and Cultural Activities : Connected with different social and human rights organisations to promote the welfare of poor, children and women; providing free legal aid to the poor and working for the protection of human rights; organised various health camps for mothers and children.

Special Interest : Protecting human rights.

Favourite Pastimes : Writing books and songs; painting and music.

INDEX

H

I

J

K

L

M

Y

Z